FREDERICK HASTINGS RINDGE

HAPPY DAYS

IN

Southern California

BY

FREDERICK HASTINGS RINDGE

CAMBRIDGE, MASSACHUSETTS
AND
LOS ANGELES, CALIFORNIA

REDEDICATION — 1984

To the memory of the author, Frederick H. Rindge, and to the reading pleasure of millions of others who have been attracted to Southern California since 1898 to savor those qualities of life unique to the Southern California coastal area that truly make day to day living a happy, rewarding experience.

I
INTRODUCTION TO THIRD PRINTING OF "HAPPY DAYS IN SOUTHERN CALIFORNIA"

LIFE IN SOUTHERN CALIFORNIA in the latter half of the 1890's was much different than that experienced in the present 1980's if your point of reference is population count, miles of roads, buildings or man-made utilitarian products such as the automobile, telephones, television, airplanes or a plethora of electronic gadgets. If, however, you can remove the man-made influences from your perspective and simply concentrate on those natural attributes of Southern California, you will find the same ingredients for enjoyable living that existed in the 1890's still exist in the 1980's. In fact, the experiences and qualities of Southern California living recounted in this book are the factors behind the heavy migration into the Southland. Thousands have sought and will continue to seek the treasures of this land glowing as a beacon light to the masses sequestered in more arduous and less attractive geographic locales.

This book captures the essence of living in Southern California. Take it and slip away to a quiet nook somewhere. Turn off the television,

INTRODUCTION

hi-fi, dishwasher and other gadgets and ensconce yourself in a comfortable reading chair. Do let your pet dog or cat join you in your retreat. If it be possible, position yourself near a window with a view of the sea or the mountains where the sun rises or sets. If it is cold, a roaring fire in a nearby fireplace will warm your spirit. Allow yourself an hour or longer for each reading—some have become so enthralled with the experiences and scenes described in this book that they've not relinquished possession till every word has been digested.

You will probably find several favorite passages that touch you personally. Whether your favorite reading be "The Storm," during a rare, intense Southern California storm, or "Ranch Life," at times you long for a closeness to the land, or other meaningful passages, you will likely experience a communion in spirit with the author of an earlier era who, like you, could never forget his "Happy Days in Southern California."

The Adamson Family
The Rindge Families
By RONALD L. RINDGE

II
Frederick H. Rindge—A Biography

FREDERICK HASTINGS RINDGE was born at Cambridge, Massachusetts, December 21, 1857, the son of Samuel Baker and Clarissa (Harrington) Rindge, of a family who migrated to America in 1638. His father was a thrifty, successful shipping merchant and banker in the Boston-Cambridge area, who amassed a sizeable estate through qualities of intelligence, diligence and perseverance applied during his business life. The author was the fourth child of six children born to his parents and the only child who survived to adulthood. The loss of two children before he was born, two more when he was four years old and his youngest brother, at age eight, when Frederick was seventeen, were events that caused his parents to carefully nurture the health and education of their only surviving child. These losses must have instilled in the author an intense appreciation of how fragile life was and how important it was to live a life of practical, beneficent actions to be sure that his stewardship over the time allotted to him was of the highest order. His religious beliefs, his writings, his business interests and his philanthropy all bear the mark of an intense belief and trust in God and that his place in the life hereafter would be assured by living according to Christian principles.

Mr. Rindge's early education was in the private schools of Boston and Cambridge and under tutors. This formal scholastic program was supplemented by broader educational and social experiences gained by extensive travel in Europe and the United States between 1870 and 1875, at which time he entered Harvard University. An illness in his senior year at Harvard forced him to spend most of that year in Florida, but he was later graduated as a member of the Class of 1879. During the next few years he traveled in Europe, America and the Sandwich Islands and worked in a Boston Commission House. His father died in 1883 and his mother died two years later. In 1887, at the age of 29, he inherited an estate of $3,000,000.00. On May 27, 1887 he married Rhoda May Knight of Trenton, Michigan and he and his wife moved to California.

The year 1887 was the year Frederick Hastings Rindge assumed many new responsibilities. His marriage brought to him the responsibilities of husband, potential parent and steward over the estate left to him by his father. After moving to California with his bride, Mr. Rindge made a succession of gifts to the City of Cambridge in memory of his father and in the spirit of contributing to the future education and government of the people of his family's native city. In the last seven months of 1887, at the age of 29, Mr. Rindge donated land and funds for a Public

A BIOGRAPHY

Library, a City Hall and an Industrial School to be initially known as the Cambridge Manual Training School for Boys—now known as the Rindge Technical School. These acts of philanthropy were accompanied by Mr. Rindge's request that a number of inscriptions be made on the buildings, and that no reference be made to him. The primary inscriptions on each building reflect the personal creeds of the author and are the reason the author referred to these as his "didactic public buildings."

The Public Library has five inscriptions—the fourth inscription reads: "It is noble to be pure; it is right to be honest; it is necessary to be temperate; it is wise to be industrious; but to know God is best of all." Over the main entrance to the City Hall is the inscription; "God has given commandments unto men. From these commandments men have framed laws by which to be governed. It is honorable and praiseworthy faithfully to serve the people by helping to administer these laws. If the laws are not enforced, the people are not well governed." The Rindge Technical School bears the following inscription: "Work is one of our greatest blessings; everyone should have an honest occupation."

The current headmaster of Rindge Technical School, Mr. Robert R. Sweeney, attests that the memory of Frederick Hastings Rindge is still a vivid one in Cambridge despite the passing of two generations. The Rindge Technical School was the first manual training school in Massachusetts and the prototype of the tech schools now flourishing across the United States. Mr. Sweeney has observed that . . . "Mr. Rindge was eighty years ahead of his time. He wanted boys to learn how to form and join metals and wood—to have a knowledge of drawing and electricity—and finally to be capable in the areas of language, mathematics and science. This allowed students trained in this manner to choose whether they would continue their education or devote themselves to careers in the trades. Consequently, you can say Mr. Rindge sensed the direction through which we became a society structured on technology. Today, the number of schools which follow the Rindge concept number in the thousands, even though many of them know nothing about Frederick Hastings Rindge."

In 1888 the author founded the Children's Island Sanitarium, donating the island of approximately 20 acres with a resort hotel for the reception and care of the sick. The only stipulation made in the gift of the island was that "no condition of race, religious faith or class should ever be introduced in the terms of admission." In 1894 and 1896 Mr. Rindge loaned his extensive collection of implements used by native races to the Peabody Museum of Archaeology and Ethnology at Harvard University, and shortly thereafter loaned a collection of over 5800 coins to the Museum of Fine Arts in Boston. These collections attest to his interest in the history of man and the practical aspects of man down through the centuries. Cornelius C. Vermeule III, Curator of Classical Art at the Boston Museum of Fine Arts, recently commented that . . . "Mr. Rindge's collecting activities among the aboriginal settlements of the Pacific Coast were those of a true pioneer, since this aspect of archaeology is so much in fashion nowadays." As to the coin collection housed in the Museum of Fine Arts, Mr. Vermeule observed, "It would seem that Mr. Rindge must have acquired much of the collection from banks dealing in foreign exchange when he worked in a Boston Commission House. The fact that he assembled hundreds of very common, circulating coins made him a true numismatist, however, for he was in advance of his time in eschewing rarity (gold and large silver, for instance) for the coins which were most apt to reach a thriving port such as Boston in every day exchange."

The above details the philanthropic activities of the author on the Atlantic Seaboard after moving to Los Angeles in 1887. His activities in Southern California were busy, progressive, beneficial and productive. He built a home on Ocean Avenue in Santa Monica. His role as husband expanded to that of parent as three children were born; Samuel Knight Rindge, Frederick Hastings Rindge, Jr. and Rhoda Agatha Rindge. He acquired the Rancho Malibu from Don Mateo Keller, a Spanish land grant extending northwesterly 20 miles from Las Flores Canyon (northwest of Santa Monica), which was later extended to approximately 25 coastal miles varying in depth of one to three miles inland from the Pacific Ocean. He built a large home in Malibu Canyon which served as headquarters for his Malibu Ranch. Between 1889 and 1902 he wrote several books, all privately printed. These books were meditative and religious in nature, except his book "Happy Days in Southern California," published in 1898, that relates his experiences of living on his Malibu Ranch and the attributes of Southern California in general.

In addition to his books of a religious vein, Mr. Rindge's interest in religion was manifested by other deeds. His personal life included prayer and Bible readings with his entire family. He erected the First Methodist Episcopal Church of Santa Monica and was active in the founding of Sunday schools on the frontier and other remote places. He was a staunch supporter of the temperance movement as exemplified in his agreement to pay from his own funds any deficit caused to the Treasury of the City of Santa Monica as a result of the loss of saloon license fees when Santa Monica abolished saloons. He was also the President of the Young Men's Christian Association of California.

Frederick Hastings Rindge was active and prosperous in business. His business investments were directed toward social and economic progress and he was quick to identify those businesses that would prosper with adequate capital and good management as they provided services, products or land that would be in great demand in future years. He founded and was president of the Conservative Life Insurance Company which is now the Pacific Mutual Life Insurance Company. He invested in Union Oil Company and Southern California Edison Company at a time when only those with far-reaching vision could see the role that petroleum and electric power would have in expanding man's capabilities and productivity. His land investments included reclamation of bottom lands near Stockton and real estate developments in San Fernando Valley and in the State of Sinaloa, Mexico.

He was president of Harvard Club of Los Angeles from its inception until his death. He was a member of the New England Historical and Genealogical Society, the Archaeological Institute of America, the Society of Colonial Wars and the Sons of the Revolution—all organizations that mirrored his interests. He was proud of his American heritage and of his forbears. His works in word and deed portray a man who was grateful for his life and who used his time and possessions to help those less fortunate than he and to support those civic, religious, social and business institutions that were necessary for building a solid, productive life for those coming after him.

Mr. Rindge spent his summers in Marblehead, Massachusetts, where the entire family made the journey by train. It was not until 1894 that he and his wife witnessed the structures he had donated to the City of Cambridge in 1887. In 1903 the Malibu Ranch home was destroyed by fire. He built a home on Harvard Boulevard in Los Angeles in 1904 and this home was declared an historical-cultural monument on February 23, 1972 by the Los Angeles Cultural Heritage Board.

Frederick Hastings Rindge died on August 29, 1905 at Yreka, California after a brief illness. The contemporary evaluation of his life and the sense of loss experienced by the community he left behind is summed up by an editorial in the *Los Angeles Times* the day after his death:

THE DEATH OF MR. RINDGE

It sincerely can be said that the death of Mr. Frederick H. Rindge has left a gap such as is seldom caused by the passing of a citizen to a higher life. Mr. Rindge's activities were so great and so constant, his sympathies were so broad and so practical, his interests were so many and so varied, his philanthropy reached so far and so wide, that his loss will be keenly felt by very many people and in very many good works.

As a business man, as a church leader, as a YMCA president, as a consistent worker for the development of the City and State, Mr.

A BIOGRAPHY

Rindge made himself so useful, that no other man can readily take his place. He was a very rich man, but he employed his wealth for the greatest good of the greatest number, not in selfish pleasure nor for personal aggrandizement. He was a man of strong religious convictions; but the grace of humility and a broad understanding prevented his religion from degenerating into religiosity. A staunch, steadfast, unassuming man, with all his millions, those who differed from him in opinion could admire his fidelity to his ideas; and those not blessed with money could be glad that such a great fortune was entrusted to such worthy hands. Men who knew Mr. Rindge best say his first aim was to do right and his next purpose was to be helpful. It is to his credit that he was discriminating in his helpfulness and would not hastily commit himself to unripe projects or untried beneficiaries.

His was a grand and lofty character, in the best sense of the terms. He helped make the world move and helped make it better. They are mourning for him this morning on the shores of the Atlantic as well as on the Pacific. Christian Civilization will have a well marked niche for him in its memoirs. Progress will lay a wreath on his bier.

RONALD L. RINDGE

CONTENTS

CONTENTS

HAPPY DAYS IN SOUTHERN CALIFORNIA

INTRODUCTION

TWO CONVERSATIONS

"Do you like Southern California?" said a Bostonian to a Santa Monican, as they were sitting together in the quietness of a pleasant little room with all the prim cosiness of a real old-fashioned New England interior, having its own peculiar individuality. The room was not cosmopolitan; it was not a museum. It was a restful room, with good cheer combined. The walls were not so covered that the eye and mind in vain sought a resting-place where one could look without being obliged to think. Too many pictures in a room deny its occupant mental rest. Whichever way he looks he sees something which sets his mind at work upon a mass of thoughts the pictures suggest. Sometimes a journey round the world is required; sometimes an historical excursion wherein the memory tries to assert its ability to recall facts and dates.

No, it was not a common abode of a man of the traveled class, without individuality, but a room in which one felt at ease, assured that its owner was well brought up, — a man whose body, soul, and mind had each grown without invading the territory of the others, and therefore not at their expense. The room did not say, "See what my master can afford; see what a surfeit of wealth I hold." Nay, it said, "My master is reflected in me; here is serenity and refinement, — not an embarrassment of riches."

The room was not like some banker's good-wife who is lost behind the glamour of her jewels, but was like that good-wife who herself adorns her apparel, whose adornment is forgotten in herself.

"Do you like Southern California?"

"Well," said the Californian, "I do love the Sunset-land. There is much to enjoy. Nature is at its best; in that new wonderland is a glorious serenity, and yet human energy is not lost as in most semi-tropical countries. It is a blending of the temperate zone with the tropic. A wonderful ocean current coming across the sea from Japan is a benediction to that coast country. Ah! Southern California is peculiar to itself!"

"Come, my good friend, tell me all about it."

"All? You ask much. I am to remain in Boston only a week. I could not tell you all

about that land were I to be your guest a
month."

"What will you write me a dozen letters for,
after you get home? You could tell me much
in them."

"For how much? Let me think. You are
an artist: paint me a figure of Christ as you
think he might have looked when he said,
'Come unto me all ye that labor and are heavy
laden, and I will give you rest.' Or, instead,
draw me an ideal countenance of a man whose
life is close to Christ, from whose face shines
the Christ-life within. Or, if you will, instead
of either, paint me a picture of a scene typical
of the thousand years of peace, — Isaiah's
prophecy, Tennyson's song. Paint in a divine
landscape with mountain background; a grove
and greensward with a silver river running to
the sea. Under the trees of the foreground
make a group of noble-countenanced people in
classic Grecian garments, all listening to a man
singing to the music of a Davidic harp, his
face upturned and glorified by breathing in the
Spirit of God. At one side of the group have
a perfect man of the millennial type, helping,
in courteous way, an aged friend to a place of
vantage that he may well hear the singing. In
a corner represent a child feeding hawks and
doves together, with the same wheat; and paint
a lamb resting and sleeping on the recumbent
form of a lion. Search the Scriptures for other

details. And above the whole scene and landscape have the Holy Ghost shine supreme, with radiating lights illuminating the picture with a supernatural glory."

"Ah," said the New Englander, "you are a Shylock to demand such a price: you could write your letters before I had my painting half finished. My palette-knife would be kept busy scraping out my attempts at the almost unattainable, while your pen would be hastening away to complete its task of possibilities."

"Very well," replied the Pacifican, "I will write a book, the writing of which will require as many hours as your picture, — you to execute your part first, notifying me of the time taken, and I will employ equal time in my portion of the contract."

The days went by. In course of time the Bostonian wrote, declaring the weeks required of me by our agreement.

But before I received word from him, I was reclining one starlight night by a campfire under a spreading live-oak in a California seaside cañon. My companion was a youth in whom I had great interest. The moon was in its first quarter, and had said good-night as it disappeared behind the hills. The sea sounds reached our ears, and the music of the brook, close by, delighted us during the hush of the waves, "like linnets in the pauses of the wind."

It was a time when two natures naturally blending become full of confidence and self-revelations. The youth had in him that sure key to knowledge, — asking questions without affront and drawing from men their experiences and memories.

He asked me about the past of the land we lived in, of the wonders of its possessions, concerning the secrets of nature, hidden in the mountains and valleys; and many another province of knowledge did he invade by his well-wrought interrogations.

Some of his questions led me soon to seek the Los Angeles Public Library and turn over many a leaf, until I had learned what I wished I had better known that summer night by the brookside.

Thus, my good reader, did these two conversations cause me to write the chapters that follow. By answering the inquiries of the Bostonian and of the youth at one and the same time, I thought I could kill two birds with one stone; although I trust I shall not kill two men with one book.

There may be those who would not decline an evening or two by the home hearth in company with me. So many love Southern California that there may be others beside the artist, the youth, and myself, who will be interested in these little stories which now begin.

SOUTHERN CALIFORNIA

THE entrances to California are enchanting, whether you approach it through the peerless Golden Gate, the doorway of one of the world's greatest harbors, or by the majestic Shasta region, its sublimity emphasized by the loveliness of the trickling streams falling over the mossy banks thereabout. Or if you enter the golden land through the attractive green valleys of Southern California, you find them rich in orange orchards and blessed with a mild, gentle air, — the vale of San Gabriel standing forth preëminent among others, themselves as fair as Cashmere, with a charm all the greater because of contrast with the arid deserts which precede them. Or, again, if you approach California over the scenic wonderlands along the Pacific railways that surmount the Rocky and Sierra Nevada ranges, there are the never-to-be-forgotten glimpses of Donner Lake through the apertures of the snow-sheds, and there abides the magnificence of the glorious view from "Cape Horn;" there you pass through the pristine pineries that cover the mountains as completely as growing grain covers a field, making one fancy that ages ago the Creator,

seated upon a floating cloud, sowed the seeds
of the pines just as a sower sows the grain.

Beautiful are thy gates, O California !

Southern California is a country of which it
is said that if a man lives there for five years
he will never leave it to stay. So, you see, it
must be a goodly land. But what are the reasons, the conditions, that make it so beloved,
that compel such loyalty to it ? They are these,
— climate, beauty, and variety. Its climate is
almost perfect, its natural attractiveness certain, and the variety of its topography remarkable. What think you of taking a sleigh ride
on Mount Lowe in the morning, descending on
a marvelous inclined railway to Pasadena, where
you stop long enough to gather your pockets
full of oranges off the trees, and then electric-
ally speeding away to Santa Monica for a swim
in the Ocean of Peace, — and all in the same
day ? Yes, it *is* true. I know of no other country in the world where such variety exists, in
such a compact area.

Southern California's history is a story, its
individuality is a poem, while life within its
borders is a delight. Unlike Italy, southern
France, Florida, and Hawaii, it has a climate
which surprises the stranger who abides all
the year round, inasmuch as the summer and
winter, the spring and autumn, here offer more
inducements to a healthful, happy, out-of-door

life than in any other locality. A small part of Chile, to be sure, has a like faultless clime, but no United States of America laws and customs add to its inherent attractions. Italy is on an inland sea, while this south-land breathes in vitality from an ocean. Hawaii inhales the air of the same sea, but that country is too near the equator for energy, and Anglo-Saxons there have to go up to San Francisco every few years, "to get their blood thickened," as they say in Honolulu. Florida, with all its loveliness, has not the priceless combination of lofty mountains and a boundless sea in close companionship. The people here breathe ozone and rarefied mountain air.

> Blow, ye winds, and bring to me
>   A breeze of hope from yonder sea.
> Change, ye zephyrs, that I may know
>   The mountain air from heights of snow.

And the winds do change, as the days go by, first giving you a thought of the Pacific and then a memory of mountains.

Many think of Southern California as a winter-land only. How can I correct that mistake? I know. Some friends of ours went to Europe in May: they returned to America in the summer-time, intending to pass some weeks on the Atlantic seaboard. But they suffered exceedingly from the hot days and more trying nights, until finally they exclaimed, "Let us go back to Southern California and get

cool!" Yes, the summer nights here are cool
and comfortable, and on our coast summer-time
is only surpassed by winter-time.

The climate here is especially restful and
strengthening to the nervous system, but it
does not enervate as do most nerve-resting
climates. Another feature of it is its remarkable power of adding weight to the body. A
certain Massachusetts man, who clung to the
platform of a Pullman, shivering in his lean-
ness and his six-feet ulster, while crossing the
Continental Divide, now dwells in San Francisco, weighing so much that I should not care
to meet him in combat. Aye, the climate pro-
motes longevity. To a great age lived many
of the native race. Victorianno, a native chief,
lived to be one hundred and thirty-six. And,
since the head that wears the crown is supposed to be troubled with insomnia, is it not
natural to believe his subjects lived to be two
hundred, at least?

It is a pleasant thought to recall the well
known resemblance of this land to Palestine.
Its climate, its topography, the course and the
times of its seasons, and its productions are all
so like the natural conditions of that holy land
that the Bible read here becomes much more
vivid.

Hesperian days long linger here, — not alone
the shortest days of the year, but nearly all the
time. Here, as in honored Palestine, God

seems to have shown his power in widely different ways, as seen in smiles of love revealed in beautiful landscapes, and then anon in his just wrath exhibited in the towering, rugged mountain steeps.

A perfect day is no rarer in March than in June. These golden days, in which the temperature of the air seems exactly to blend with the conditions of the body, are not hard to find, and I am glad he who wrote "what so rare as a day in June?" lived not here, for then would the world have missed that sweet song.

Southern California, like Korea, might be called the Land of the Morning Calm, because our mornings are so serene and pleasant, before the trade-winds begin to blow, — from noon till sundown.

When the "Morning Times" declares the destitution and suffering in snow-bound cities, then are we grateful that our lines have been cast in pleasant places, in this the land of green Christmas-tide, in this Southern California, the winter fireside of our country.

The happiest thought of all thoughts in connection with this beautiful land is that only in Heaven is it more beautiful, and that we can live there, too, if we are faithful.

So dear has Southern California become to thousands of transplanted citizens that they feel like exclaiming, in the words of the legend attached to the old California Republic silk

flag preserved in the museum of the Pioneers'
Society of San Francisco, —

"California is ours as long as the stars remain."

What need I say more to substantiate her
claim to be called the Golden State? Do not
the golden orange, and the golden nugget,
and the golden native poppy, God-given, prove
the justice of her assertion?

In the chapters that ensue permit me to pass
by in silence those great resorts that have delighted the traveler.

Instead, it is my hope to tell of those things
that are sometimes forgotten; and especially
do I hope so to write that if some of you knew
not the title of this book and saw no proper
names therein, you would at once say, "He is
surely writing about Southern California."

So, come, my mind! pray serve me once
again; and thou! my good right hand, obey the
brain, thy master, and breathe into this book
the serenity of Southern California: color these
chapters with a semi-tropical tinge, a veritable
verbal-colored photograph, if thou wilt; and
make my words bear a balmy breeze from the
Ocean of Peace to those who may wish to know
thee or renew memories of thy clime of climes,
O Southern California!

OUR FIRST PREDECESSORS

LET us go to some cañon which leads from the mountains to the sea, and whose mouth is a broad open valley facing the beach; such as is the old Santa Monica, or the Malibu, or fair Zuma.

It is a bright spring morning. Everything is growing. The fragrance of the musky alfilaria perfumes the air. Canoes are returning from their early fishing; a group of aborigines are engaged in digging clams at the lower-low tide. When the tide returns and stops this occupation, they will begin to open the tightly closed shells by a clever trick. They will put them on a bed of coals, the clam opens his shell when he feels the heat, and the watching Indian, ready with a sharp stick, quickly pries it open. On the beach a company of happy-hearted children are awaiting the canoes, running and playing on the sands: the older boys, with guatamote and sagebrush bows and arrows, showing their skill in shooting at peep and plover, while the older girls sit braiding baskets. Up the beach a man is gathering asphaltum, washed ashore by the tide from the depths of the sea, with which to cover the

braided baskets and bottles the girls are making, in order that they may be water-tight.

Up on the mesa above we see the village
site; the fires in front of the little huts are
still smoking; the mothers are tending their
children, drying venison, and with pestles are
preparing food seeds and acorns in the mortars.   Others make tortillas on a permanent
metate on the top of a ledge.   These, with
cooked seal flippers and porpoise meat, make
up their ordinary food.   Some of the mortars
are chiseled out of bed rock or great above-
ground ledges, while others are finely wrought
vessels.

On the trail which comes down from the
heights towards Calabasas we see a party of
hunters homeward-bound with the deer slain
in the daybreak hunt.   Some of the young
men on the trail bring back a fine number of
sweet-tasting quail, caught in the cunning basket and brush-chute traps.

Here is their little primitive world.   Here
their love-matches are made; here Pacific Hia-
wathas honor their tribe; here in fear of war
and in love of life they spend their years.
From this mesa, or level hilltop, they carry
down their dead to the little cemetery by the
lake.

On the point of the mesa do you see that
white-locked warrior peering out to sea, with
his hand held to shield his eyes, to discern

the meaning of a fleet of canoes in the distance? In his left hand he carries a seven-foot staff, which is pointed by a well-made obsidian stone spearhead, eight inches long : this is the symbol of his power as chief. With earnestness does he scan the sea. Is it war ahead? Or is it the approach of the cruel Russians, who kill the islanders to get their otter-skin clothing, finding this method easier than hunting the otter in the sea? Nay, those are trading canoes which have come from the north with treasures of obsidian and rare baskets and cherished ornaments ; food products also they bring, the fancy groceries of the past.

Earlier in the morning, at sunrise, we could have seen some of the devout on an eminence near by, worshiping, in attitudes of adoration and supplication, the Great Spirit.

But all is astir when the trading canoes come into the little bay and are beached on the willing sand. An unfinished courtship is now to be renewed, and a troth pledged.

The southern maiden quietly sits aside, skillfully cutting out abalone ornaments and piercing the pieces with little drills ; out of them she will make necklaces of shell, and decorative beads. She waits : she will soon know if her beloved from the north will seek her out from among the many, and, passing by the more forward maids, honor her.

Yes, he has not forgotten : she has been his,

in his heart, away up in the distant northland.
See! his haste proves his love: he has brought
her a treasure of northern gifts. Among other
things, he brings her a Klamath basket, delicately woven and interwoven in ingenious pat-
terns with yellow-hammer feathers and quail
crests; and look! the basket is full of shining
Pescadero pebbles. With sweet modesty she
gives him a perfect blossom of the bell-shaped
sand-flower, — the sacred flower of her race.
God bless them both!

We leave them to their happiness. Others
of the tribe are leaving the village with willow
striking-fans and baskets to gather the food
seeds from the hills, in the chaparral.

Do you notice? they strike the ripe seed
pods and the seeds fall into the baskets held
underneath. Still others go forth to pick up
the ripe acorns, to replenish their granary,
while yon woman is going down the trail to
the little brook in the cañon to fill her water-
bottles.

In the village some of the older men are
mixing and preparing medicine. The elder-
berry root steeped is their powerful purgative,
the berries of the bearberry-tree are their emetic,
while the wormwood and sage serve as their
febrifuge.

The most skillful of the women are busy
making fine arrow and spear points out of
chalcedony, smoky topaz, serpentine, chert, and

crystal quartz, for we are observing a people advanced in honor and chastity above the Diggers and Modocs and most other primitive men, whose finely chipped instruments and other workmanship excel most of the aboriginal work on our continent. We must not forget that aged one of the tribe. To her is intrusted the fashioning of the great war-dance costume : her great pride is the helmet of this, made of closely woven grasses, impervious to the average arrow, and crowned or crested with road-runners' tail-feathers. The garment itself is made of grasses and feathers interwoven, and decorated with bright-colored abalone ornaments.

So they pass their lives till Cabrillo's white-winged ships approach. Rumors of Cortes have come from the south, borne from tribe to tribe, from Mexico to Malibu. The ancient telegraph here was the voice of man. Cortes' horses had been described and probably exaggerated. The ships of the Spaniards had been described, and their weapons of war, holding thunder and death-dealing, had prepared our first predecessors for the sight of Cabrillo's ships, now sailing into Santa Monica Bay.

A sudden secret knell sounded in their hearts. One glance at the ships struck awe in their souls. They read their doom in the ship, the horse, and the gunpowder. Man always stands in awe of what he himself cannot make or do.

Montezuma's name had been known from Mexico to Point Duma and beyond. If he, the Great Aztec, could be conquered and Mexico left unprotected by their God of War, what help was there for the smaller Zuma tribe or the others along the coast ?

Many a council held the men of battles. Varied was the advice of the old men and leaders. Some were for peace, some for aggressive war. But all felt as if they were battling with something akin to the supernatural.

It was this supernatural idea which made the aborigines a readier prey to the Spaniards. Curiosity, too, played its part : the Indian was as eager to see the thunder-guns as is an antelope to learn the cause of a waving handkerchief in the daytime on the plains, or a lantern near the lick at night.

Besides, Cabrillo came and went, not with destruction, but with kindness. When he first came, a report of his coming was taken from tribe to tribe up the coast, and the headlands were covered by eager, awed watchers. Let us leave them there.

But whence came they, these aborigines ? Of course the primal answer must be, that they are only a part of the human race once scattered at the time of the Tower of Babel. To trace the migrations of these aboriginal people, and to discover what paths they took to enter our present domains, is a much more difficult question.   The Chinese lay claim, from their ancient records, to the discovery of America.   In the Harvard University collections is a jade cup found in Central America, identical in appearance and specific gravity with Chinese jade, none being found in America, I believe, approaching it.   Moreover, the hieroglyphs on certain rocks in Central America are said to be akin to Chinese characters.   I have an ancient earthen idol with great tusks, from Honduras; I am inclined to think its maker must have come from Hindustan.

I doubt not the civilization of ancient Mexico and Central America was a complex one; formed, perhaps, by a blending of the life of the lost continent of Atlantis, together with Asiatic influences brought across the sea from China and India, and down the coast from Japan *via* the Aleutian Islands.   Indeed, I have an Indian slate-stone dish or plaque, carved in relief, with a representation of three natives battling with an octopus which has upset their canoe and is seeking to devour the men; it bears evidences of early Japanese art. Then again certain walrus ivory carvings and etchings in my collection betray Japanese influence.

To return to our Indian village in long-ago Southern California.   I see and hear at night, about the smouldering fire, the Nestor of the tribe telling stories of the past.   He relates

how, on the coast to the north of the great
bay, a strange canoe, of great size and having
mighty wings, was wrecked on the rocks, and
how heavy (metal) ropes, and figures made of
heavy substance (metal) washed ashore ; and
how the dead men found on the beach were
unlike any men that had ever been seen.

This vision is no idle dream ; for on the
Oregon coast very ancient bronze cables and
idols have been found in the beach sands.
Some of these are now in the Museum of the
State Mineralogical Bureau at San Francisco.

I remember when we found a memorial of
these our first predecessors, — an ancient cave-
dwelling, with its smoke-darkened ceiling and
its heaps of débris and shells round about, the
remains of a thousand feasts.

SPANISH DAYS

CABRILLO was the first Spaniard who sailed along the shores of Southern California. It was in 1542. From him, and successive explorers, the Spanish learned about our fertile valleys, the delightful climate, and the abundance of wild game and fish food; and how numerous were the dusky people that then inhabited our lands.

So that when, in 1767, a general expulsion of the Jesuits occurred from Spanish countries, the Jesuits resolved to enter our California as a mission field. This they did, under the spiritual leadership of Padre Junipero Serra, whose own crucifix is still preserved in the sacristy of the old church at Monterey.

In 1769 they planted the first mission at San Diego, and in succeeding years their missions were established to the north as far as Sonoma, above San Francisco, which was built in 1823. The stations were placed at average intervals of twelve leagues. It was in 1821 that they obtained their greatest glory.

The Spanish priests came with bell and book, incense and incantation, — things well suited to the sensuous Indian nature. Soon the awe

which the aborigines felt for the Europeans
was trained into obedience. The mission
buildings rose. The herds of cattle and other
stock now made their beginning. Olive orchards, vineyards, and wheat fields after a while
yielded their increase. Rude manufactures
were started. America was being gradually
changed into Europe.

Soon after the priests, soldiers and artisans
came. Intermarriages resulted, and the two
races began to blend.

Not all was peace. Some tribes, Apache-
like, refused to relinquish freedom for what
they thought was slavery. They observed that
all the mission buildings were built by native
labor, under the direction of the Spaniards. So
the guns and machetes from Spain had plenty
of defensive work to do. But in the course
of time, as the children were taught European
ways and the catechism of the Spaniard's faith,
the country became more peaceful. The people from the settlements would go out into the
mountains and serve as peacemakers.

The names of places you meet with in California which ante-date the coming of the Anglo-
Saxons were in many cases bestowed by Cabrillo and Serra. As his ship sailed along the
coast, Cabrillo would look at his almanac, when
he sighted a promontory or other noteworthy
natural feature, and give it the name of the saint
on whose day the discovery was made. Then

he would enter it upon the chart he was making. Other names, like Guadalasca, betray their
Moorish origin, and carry one far back into the
Spanish past. Still other names, as Hueneme,
are of Indian dialect ; it is said this word means
" a house by the sea."

In the Lompoc valley are the ruins of an old
mission. This structure was never completed
because the occurrence of an earthquake, by
which a portion of the building under construction fell to the ground, was unwisely deemed
of ill portent to the enterprise.

Consecrated bells were held in the greatest
esteem in those days. If a ship sailed from
Mexico to San Diego with one such on board,
her safe arrival in port was assured ; and ex-
peditions inland always were thought to be well
planned if a priest and a bell went with them.
On making a camp, the bell would be hung on
a branch of some great tree. I have been told
that the tree under which mass was first said
on the banks of Los Angeles River, and from
which the holy bell hung, was still standing in
1892 ; but my informant, who recently sought
to secure it for historical purposes, found it had
been cut up by a Mexican for stove-wood !

Before closing this chapter let us consider
Coronado a moment. You come across his
name often in Southern California. Coronado
was governor of a Mexican province. In 1540
he was dispatched with an expedition to dis-

cover, up in what is now New Mexico, "the seven cities of Cibola, full of gold," the existence of which had been reported by a friar who had traveled far into the interior. These fabled golden cities seem to have been nothing more than Zuñi pueblos, — Indian towns, terraced, built of stone. Distant cities are always golden, as distant pastures are green.

Coronado's men even marched to the Grand Cañon of the Colorado. Think of this when you look upon that triumph of God.

THE MEXICAN ERA

In 1821 Mexico gained her independence. By this time the Spanish blood had become so intermingled with that of the native races that those who called themselves Spanish were no longer Spanish, but rather Europeanized Aztecs. Since their blood was mostly Aztec, they could not now submit to Spain, after the awe had worn away. Awe in man vanishes when he can do the same things as those whom he once reverenced because of his ignorance. Besides, the Spaniards did not always practice what they preached.

Under valiant and noble leaders, Mexican independence became a fact, and Southern California shared in its benefits. To the Mexicans here residing their Independence Day is as dear as our Fourth of July is to us.

The greatest change that came to Southern California through Mexican independence was the secularization of the missions. As the Jesuits had been driven out of Spain in 1767, so now were they expelled from Mexico. The Southern California mission churches were intrusted to the Franciscans and Dominicans.

This act of the secularization of the missions

resulted in their downfall.   Southern California
now changed from a priest-controlled community to a civilization which might be called
semi-democratic, or one in which the state was
put above the church.

The Mexican governors now held sway.   And
the influence of the great landowners of Mexican grants was powerful.

It is interesting for the stranger to know
that nearly all Southern Californian land titles
go back to Mexican grants which, on the purchase of California by the United States, were
approved by the United States patents.   These
grants consisted of thousands of acres of land
each.   Sometimes they were given by the government to reward military service, or for religious foundations, or for pueblo purposes;
and sometimes they were sold.   Each "grant"
had a distinctive name, like Jesu-Maria, or San
Antonio, — or Topango, or Malibu, or Sequit,
named from aboriginal tribes.

The mission buildings, except the churches
themselves, went to gradual decay.   The cattle
of San Gabriel Mission in 1821 numbered
100,000.   But after the secularization of the
missions, their various estates having been sold
for two million dollars, the great herds were
scattered or slaughtered and the vineyards went
to waste, in many cases.

The large Mexican land grants of fifty thousand acres, more or less, were made to prominent

Mexicans, mostly as rewards for military service. Now such holders began to develop their properties. Cattle, horses, and sheep were about the only means they knew of getting an income from their lands. To be sure, corn, some cereals, olives, and grapes brought them some money, or rather supplies; but with their great natural resources they did but little in a commercial sense. No trade or commerce had they to speak of, largely because they lacked transportation facilities. Had they been Anglo-Saxons they would have found a market, and a way to reach it.

In this Mexican epoch was the hide and tallow trade developed. Dana's "Two Years Before the Mast" paints its picture. Cattle were raised not for their meat chiefly, but for their hides and tallow. In those days, if a traveler were hungry he could kill a steer, but he must hang the hide on a tree for the owner. Nowadays some wicked Americans not only steal the meat, but bury the hide, so that the owner gets neither. May their tribe decrease!

Unbounded hospitality and generosity prevailed among the Mexicans, especially at the large ranchos, where the landowners had under them great numbers of employees and dependents. Travelers were furnished fresh horses gratuitously, and "to give to him that asketh" was a principle they put into practice.

Their life was the essence of the Spanish

proverb, "If you work to live, what is the use of working yourself to death?" But there is a purpose in life not to be lost in foolish folklore. Yet a little of this proverb could be well applied by some of our countrymen. Others of them are lazy anyway, and do not need it.

We wish we had time to talk together about their adobe homes and sunny porches, their horsemanship, their clumsy carts, their barbecues, their table supplies, and boiled mustard "for greens," their cruel bullfights when chile-pepper was put in the slit tongues of the already enraged beasts to increase their fury and add excitement to the undesirable zest of the gathering; about the bandit raids, about their rodeos, and concerning their religious rites, and their customs in honor of the patron saint of the crops and fields, San Ysidro, and also of their dry-year processions when rain was invoked from Heaven. Perhaps we will talk over these things when we meet again.

But the Mexican epoch is ending. The Mexican war has been raging, and can you not hear Don Pio Pico telling his friend how General Frémont is marching down the coast on Southern California; how the Mexicans had expected he would pass through the Gaviota Cañon, where great boulders had been brought to roll down upon him and to crush his men; and how the rascally gringo got word of it and went around by a mountain pass?

THE COMING OF THE WHITE MEN

THE Mexican war, between the United States of America and Mexico, lasted from 1846 to 1848. One of the results of that war was the purchase of California, by our country, from Mexico.

Before this time there had been some Anglo-Saxons in California. A member of the Packard family is said to have settled here in 1780. The first of our trading ships that entered San Francisco harbor was the Eagle, Captain William H. Davis, from Boston, who came via Hawaii and Alaska in 1816. And from this time on until the Mexican War the love of adventure had brought quite a number of white men to these shores.

In 1846 Commodore Sloat raised our flag at Monterey, to bear witness that the United States had occupied California. But it is said the first American flag ever raised in California flew to the breeze on Fremont's Peak, overlooking the town of Hollister. The first flag made in California was made by a daughter of Don Juan Bandini, who afterward became Mrs. Carrillo.

From the time of the purchase of California

until its admission into the Union as a State it was under a provisional government.   Admission Day in California is a legal holiday, and a great day.

It is related that General Tecumseh Sherman was, in his younger years, sent West with an engineer corps to make surveys of our newly bought California. When he returned to Washington to make his report, he went to see President Taylor.

Mellville D. Landon states the conversation between them as follows : —

"'Glad to see you, Sherman : seen all the new land, have you ?'

"'Yes, and surveyed it all.'

"'Well, how do you like our new possessions ?'

"'Well — a — I — t-h-i-n-k,' — and then Sherman scratched his head in deep thought.

"'What !' exclaimed the President, 'you don't say you don't like them ?'

"'Well, I am afraid, — I'm afraid, Mr. President, we've got to have another war with Mexico.'

"'Another war ? Why, what for ?'

"'To make them take the country back.'"

President Taylor and General Sherman would be astounded to-day if they could take a trip over the kite-shaped track on the Santa Fé in Southern California, — to say nothing of the kingdom above Tehachapi.

In September, 1846, certain Californians under Flores and Varela revolted, and captured Los Angeles after a siege. Gillespie, in command at Los Angeles, sent a dispatch to Stockton, at San Francisco, informing him of his danger. This dispatch was carried on horseback by Juan Flaco, who made the distance of six hundred miles in five days.

While the ride of Paul Revere and that of Sheridan have been immortalized in verse by Longfellow and Read, Juan Flaco's ride, of equal heroism and greater endurance and danger, still awaits the poet.

I think I know a man who would give a prize to the poet who would do justice to Juan Flaco — John the Thin. But no, — because if I should offer a prize it would result in an endless correspondence, and I should have to say to so many competitors that their efforts were *only* efforts, that I should wish myself an aborigine, preferring to defend myself against spearmen rather than against disappointed or unappreciated self-alleged poets.

Nevertheless, Juan Flaco's ride ought to be written.

But the coming of the white men really dates from the discovery of gold by Marshall, in 1848. Then they came in swarms by land and by sea.

It was gold, not goodness, that led the white men to seek California, — although, as the Puritans for conscience' sake sailed to New England, so to the coasts of California the first Spanish settlers came in the name of religion.

Around the Horn and over the prairies, amid many perils, came the gold-seekers ; there were not many family names in the Eastern lands but furnished one argonaut. They passed by little Los Angeles. On to the gold-fields and into the mountains, was their cry ! What was Los Angeles then, and thereafter for a long, sleepy time ? Only a source of San Francisco's cattle and sheep supply. And yet now Los Angeles and the southlands rightly claim the crown above the aspiration of the northlands. So be it, until in the character of its citizens, as a whole, the north can surpass the south.

In those days of '49 prices were great, very great. Even in the early success of Leadville, where the barber did not blush a bit to ask me seventy-five cents for a tonsorial triumph, prices did not approach the '49 days.

Marshall, who discovered gold in 1848, has left behind him his account book. He states that in 1849 a hat was worth twelve dollars, a frying-pan six dollars, a paper of tacks three dollars, one onion for a sick man sixty dollars, and flour a dollar and a quarter a pound.

But by and by, the iron horse and the steamship took the place of the ox-team and the ships that sail. The serpentine track came around a better " Cape Horn," and, turning southward, came trailing over the Tehachapi, and a kingdom was born almost in a single day. The Southern Pacific Railroad introduced the Sunset-land to the world; but it was left to the Santa Fé route to bring the thousands of guests to her union with prosperity, which she had largely brought about.

Strangers came by hundreds. They verified the reports of the unrivaled clime, which had been sent to the snow countries in the East. Their health improved. They said, It is good to be here; it is a marvelous country. They wrote home about it and thousands more came. The people were so enthusiastic about the climate's virtue that they began to think each foot of land well-nigh priceless. They were not far wrong. Thus began the great land-boom, in which fortunes were made and lost with astonishing rapidity. The decade of 1880–1890 was a wonder.

The trains kept bringing in their human freights, and as "merit is the secret of success" of course Southern California continues to grow in population as few lands have grown.

The climate has been the chief cause of Southern California's success, but let it not be forgotten that the general character of her people has had as much to do with her permanent welfare.

Had it not been for the coming of the white men, this southland would perhaps never have been aroused from its lethargy; and its resources would never have been developed but for their enterprise. In Southern California, which was once a sleepy place, the coming of the Anglo-Saxon has turned inactivity into bustle. The old way was to say, " Manana sera otro dia" (To-morrow will be another day), but now it is, "Work while it is day."

BY THE SIDE OF THE SUNSET SEA

ON THE BEACH

Our seaside life is at its glory when the children from Los Angeles seek its summer shores at the times of the lower-low tides. There are the marine treasures to be found. Young life bounds and rebounds like a rubber ball, under the influence of the sea air. Then are confidences spoken among the older visitors; then are new hopes kindled. Then the ozone makes new men out of those that come from the city offices, those modern cliff-dwellers. There is a fascination in walking, riding, or driving along the untrodden sands of a stretch of beach. What may not one expect to find just around that curve in the shore, just beyond those rocks? Some curiosity, or feathery sea-fern more beautiful than any in your basket, some pebble brighter than Redondo's brightest, were that possible.

Ah yes, there are great things to be found by the sea; there are great sights to see. Do you remember when a part of the White Navy anchored off the bluff and engaged in target practice, — how the cannon boomed and the water splashed near the floating targets? How the smoke on the Monadnock was seen before the report was heard, and how we told the children that was because sound traveled more slowly than sight? How proud we were of *our* ships! In time of war it is well that our White Navy should be given a darker hue, for it seems as if the glistening white ships would make good targets for the enemy's gunners.

On the beach what exercise our eyes find, — the silvery flash of the flying beach birds, the hastening crabs escaping to the sea, the red, white, and blue jellyfish left stranded by the tide, and the prettiest starfish ever seen. In Southern California we have pink starfish, and a crab whose shell is shaped like an oak leaf. In places, also, the poisoning stingaree abounds. The points of the brittle starfish if broken off will grow out again, like the broken claws of an Atlantic lobster. How convenient it would be if human arms would grow out again after a railroad accident, when the surgeon had to amputate them at the elbow!

Now the children have found some cowrie shells; not fine great ones like those from the South Sea Islands, but real little cowries, nevertheless. They are not so handsome as the rare orange cowrie your sea-captain uncle brought from Tahiti, now reposing on the mantel; nor as beautiful as the tiger cowrie, on whose shell is often engraved the Lord's Prayer.

On the beach at Soston Cañon we once found what we thought was a baby sea turtle. We brought him home, but afterwards returned him to the sea with the request that he would grow and come back to us for green-turtle soup purposes.   He is still at large.

A Santa Monica fisherman recently found a sea turtle asleep on the waters of the bay and lifted him, unsuspecting, into the boat.   His weight was sixty-five pounds.   A green turtle killed in San Diego Bay weighed three hundred pounds ; but he was supposed to have escaped from the steamer Newbern, wrecked on the voyage from San Francisco from Lower California.

Sometimes the cañon tortoises visit the beach, and sun in the sands.   They will also go into the sea a little way.   I remember a pretty group of laughing children surrounding a tortoise.   Down the inclined plane of the beach sand made by the tides would go the tortoise, followed by the laughter of the children, who would catch him as he was about to escape into the sea and bring him back for another toboggan scamper down the incline.   Our dog Protector, too, would out-laugh the children with his bark.   The boys must have the turtle to take home with them, of course.   So they made a little corral of a bottomless box, and put him in.   After two days he burrowed out underneath the box, and had a short walk to *his* home-haunts, laughing in his sleeve, no doubt. It was *his* turn to laugh.

Is there anything in the world more awkward than a turtle trying to right himself, after you have put him on his back?

Happy memories of happy days! when the family go to the beach, and cover the children with the warm sand, to their great delight; presently, they shake themselves out of it and roll over and over down the sand-dune slants. Meanwhile their elders absorb the strengthening balm of the beach. There gently rises one of those quiet, lapping tides, when the sea looks like a floor and the little waves idly whip the shore; just right for the boys to skip stones upon. Our Saint Bernard lies on the sand and lets the gentle waves of the incoming tide wash over him. See the sea shimmering in the summer sun!

There is much virtue in beach sand. It has excellent strength-giving power for the weak. In France the aged poor resort to the warm summer sands as to a well reputed physician, since they cannot afford both; they find their strength and vitality and longevity increased thereby.

One of the children runs up to us with a starfish he has found, and, in a meditative mood, inquires if shooting stars falling into the ocean make starfishes. Again he inquires, "Do they make jelly out of jellyfishes?"

Have you ever watched the sand-hoppers boring into the beach? Did you ever examine their kicking apparatus? It is a marvel.

Yes, the seashore must have been made for children to enjoy. Amid the rocks what delights there are! The great flat rock up the coast, extending into the sea, is a natural aquarium, abounding with miniature lakes and pools of crystal water, left by the receding tide, an August paradise for children. Here the sea anenomes and sea urchins dwell in their pristine state. Mussels and barnacles are on the rocks. Here lives the blue barnacle with its jointed armadillo-like back. There are many more ideal places further up towards Point Duma, where the water is shallow and sea-life abounds.

The thoughts of the sea that come back to me are connected with the treacherous quicksands, the occasional mirage, the phantom ships, so made by the hazy horizon, half clear half foggy; the great Panama steamers plying proudly by, away out at sea, which we see sometimes indistinctly, when we try to count all the ships in sight; just as when in the early evening we count the few stars, and gradually discern some at first unseen. Did you count that British ship lying off Port Los Angeles, just in from Antwerp, one hundred and thirty days? My mind goes back to the quaint natural rocks up the coast on the beach : the standing bear, the huge sea turtle, and the pair of mighty cymbals lying half imbedded in the sand, as if left there by some old giant when he ran to save himself from a tidal wave of the past. Many a load of cottage firewood has been hauled home from the beach. Driftwood from the barranca's mouth and wreckage has cooked many a fisherman's meal. Once we found on the shore part of a lost boat, on which was carved the name, "Lóttie." It had been borne thither on the crests of countless waves from who knows where, — perhaps a sad message to some still hoping wife.

In the distance the islands — Santa Catalina (Saint Catherine's Isle), Santa Barbara, and Santa Cruz — hold up their haughty heads, proud of their victories over the storms.

On San Miguel Island, off Santa Barbara City, Juan Rodriguez Cabrillo, the first explorer of the California coast, was buried. In aboriginal days, these islands were more populous than the mainland.

But Catalina is the isle that appeals to the people. Her rock-bound coasts are jeweled with abalones: she is the queen of the sea's domain. Wonderful is she for her submarine gardens in the still waters.

The abalone shells are sent to New York to be made into buttons, and are brought back to California for sale. They should be made here and give wages to our own. But that is more honorable than shipping cottonseed oil from

New Orleans to Italy, and having it thence shipped to California as pure olive oil. It is marvelous how it is miraculously changed into pure olive by the journey!

THE OCEAN OF PEACE

It is said that if the whole of the earth's surface above water were thrown into the Pacific Ocean it would fill only one seventh of it. The average depth of this ocean is about four thousand two hundred yards. So you see you live by the side of a mighty sea.

Yon boundless ocean is the best symbol of eternity. As the blue sea receives its color from the sky above it, so can we receive the attributes of Heaven if we live under obedience to God. The deep blue sea reflects the deeper blue of the heavens : so man's goodness reflects the greater goodness of God.

By the sea the moonlight and the twilight reveal themselves with rare loveliness. The golden glimmer of the sunrise sea is of great beauty, while the sunsets supply a public picture gallery at the close of countless days in the year. Many natural attractions surround the Southern California coast.

> Accept them like the sunsets
> Which are given unto men
> To prove the sure existence
> Of a Power Sovereign.

Standing on the beach, look out upon the

swelling, round-backed ocean : so it looks over towards the horizon. Hear the swish of the tide. Listen to the round rocks, grumbling as they are rolled down the beach by a receding wave, their rest disturbed. Beware of the cruel undertow that crouches ready for its prey.

Now the incoming tide throws its long tongues of foaming water up on the beach, lapping the sands. What a variety there is by the ocean ; no wonder one of the best beloved songs is, "Oh, give me a home by the sea." Along our wave-washed coast, where the crannied many-colored sandstone cliffs wall the shore, the thunder of the boisterous surf echoes and reëchoes on the mountain sides until it seems like the roar of another ocean.

The ocean, it is said, will yield more food to the acre of good fishing-ground than an acre of the best tillage land.

How grateful to him who has been long absent is the familiar smell of the sea ! It seems to supply a new life.

How many and varied are the moods of the sea ! It has a mood to fit every mood of man. When the little waves in graceful, white-fringed curves roll gently up on the sands, one would never think the ocean capable of cruelty or anger.

> The quiet waters of the Bay
> Have ever seemed to me to say,
> In quietness is strength.

The breeze rises, and the white caps, nodding their heads on the wind-driven sea, are borne along on the wings of the tide.

> The white caps on the dark blue sea
> Little sail-boats seem to be.

The wind grows strong, and the chasing waves leap like a pack of greyhounds after a coursing hare.

Now in angry mood the roaring sea seeks to overleap its God-set bounds, as foolish unregenerate man seeks to be free from laws enacted for his good, and so becomes a slave. Hear the loud-sounding sea with its ceaseless turmoil; hear the surf, making sand, as it beats without mercy on the helpless shore. That roar is the incessant beating of the ocean's heart, in wrath. The kelp lies thick-strewn upon the beach, torn from its submarine garden.

Sometimes the fierce Santa Anna wind blows offshore, and then let the little shipping look out. This wind chops up good nature as well as the surface of the sea. The Santa Anna is not conducive to kindliness. In Spain they have a hot wind called the Solano. They have a proverb which says, "Ask no favors during Solano."

The storm has spent its fury now, and the sound of the sea is as the mighty music of a pealing anthem, or as if it were rolling a requiem for many a lost crew.

Five miles away the distant ocean seems so calm; but be in its companionship for months and you will learn that it can be cruel. And yet compared with the Atlantic, the Pacific *is* the Ocean of Peace.

CONCERNING THE SEASHORE

Reclining on the beach it is hard to believe that a tidal wave has ever occurred in Southern California. Yet such is the case. In 1855 there were great earthquakes in Japan and vicinity. These earthquakes made a tidal wave which reached our shores in thirty-eight hours. At San Diego the tide rose twelve feet in one night.

But how protected from elementary disturbances is Southern California; in Japan a recent tidal wave was eighty feet in height, rushed inland two miles and a half along two hundred miles of coast, and drowned thousands. There, about sunset, four shocks of earthquake were felt; then a terrible noise was heard from the sea, and soon the great wall of water advanced to destroy. In 1812 there was a seismic disturbance in Los Angeles.

In 1857 and in 1862 there were two California shipwrecks which startled the world. The first was the loss of the California steamship Central America, in which four hundred and fifty people were drowned, and two million dollars in gold were sunk in the sea off the cape. The men were miners returning to their Eastern homes, and the treasure consisted of the sacks of gold the men had made out of the mountains. When the ship went down many of the miners lost their reason, and their sacks of gold were strewn about the decks, while their owners frantically threw themselves into the sea.

In 1862 the Panama steamer Golden Gate, carrying several hundred passengers, and one million five hundred thousand dollars in gold bullion for the Eastern mints, took fire off the coast of Mazatlan, and was run ashore. The steamer sank, two hundred people were drowned, and the treasure was at the bottom of the sea. A company was afterwards organized to recover the treasure, and eight hundred thousand dollars was obtained.

Speaking of ships, I should not forget to give an account of the earliest shipbuilding in Southern California, which Professor Polley describes in the following words : —

" Father Sanchez, at the old San Gabriel Mission, being desirous of securing some of the spoils of sea-otter hunting, conceived the idea of building a schooner to ply around the Channel Islands and capture sea otter. The natives had no knowledge of shipbuilding. Joseph Chapman, Father Sanchez's major-domo, had been a ship carpenter in early life. He was the first English-speaking person to settle in California. He had been taken prisoner by the Californians at Ortego's Rancho when Burchard, the pirate, plundered the coast settlements. Chapman, with the assistance of the Indians at the mission, got out the timbers for the vessel, some of which were hauled from the San Bernardino Mountains. When the timbers were all framed they were mounted on huge carretas and hauled from San Gabriel to San Pedro Bay, where the vessel was put together and launched. It was two years in building. The vessel made several trips to the islands for otter. It was afterward sold and used in the coast trade between California and Mexico. It was finally wrecked."

The padres at San Gabriel used to send their Indians to the Malibu Ranch to fish and hunt, drying the fish and venison for a winter's supply. There deer were very numerous ; even in my time an old hunter related how, in Yerba Buena Cañon, he had killed forty-five deer. In a cave in Sequit Cañon Mr. M. K. Harris found a great pile of bleached antlers, placed there long ago by some hunter.

Even the sands of our seashore have a trace of gold in them. Sometimes you see much black in the sand ; that black is magnetic iron, and in conjunction with it are minute grains of gold, but not enough to make any one anxious to leave farming.

In the sand queer finds are sometimes made. Once at Monterey I took a long walk up the beach above the Hotel del Monte, and sat down to rest on the sands. Idly moving my hands through the sand I felt something hard, and, lo and behold! it was an ancient Spanish coin of the eighteenth century! Had some padre from the Monterey Mission in days of old, during a temptation, gone up the beach alone to pray, and, bending over his rosary, which he had drawn from his clothing, dropped his pocket-piece, this keepsake of old Spain?

I have read of early coins being found on the Florida coast, but never on our shores. By the way, I have a gold coin of about 1492 with the portraits of Ferdinand and Isabella thereon, to whom, in some degree, we owe Southern California.

Down near Redondo a boxed Bible once floated ashore. Clam Jack, who found it, is an old-timer who earns his living by digging clams, and peddling them out in Redondo from his faithful old burro. I have often wondered whence came that fine Bible, so carefully crated. Perhaps when some ship was going down it was thrown overboard by some one who knew its worth. It may have been a message from Heaven to kind old Clam Jack. May he have accepted the passport to God, so strangely sent.

UNDER THE SEA

Since in this book we have together walked over the mesas and climbed up the mountains, let us also take a trip over the fields at the

ocean's depths. The dredger's art, the fisherman's toil, and the glass set in the bottom of
the boat make this possible. There are strange
sights under the sea; there are busy scenes
below. The submarine topography is much the
same as the land's, even unto volcanoes, one
of which is off Cape Mendocino, another off
the coast of Chile, while nearer home fishermen have told about hot water coming to the
surface of the sea near San Clemente Island
and of submarine disturbance off San Miguel
Island.

Wherever kelp is found growing in the sea,
there expect to find a rocky bottom. From
such places under the ocean grow up in grandeur the great kelp-trees, their branches reach-
ing upward to the sun. Through these trees
of kelp the fish swim, as wood-birds fly among
the tall pines of forests. As underbrush grow
in the submarine deeps the seaweeds and
sponges; of the latter only an uncommercial
variety is ours. These seaweeds are as beautiful in design and coloring as wild-wood plants
and ferns. Indeed, some one, I know not who,
has said of these seaweeds, "Call us not
weeds; we are Ocean's gay flowers." Red starfish, colored like the planet Mars, dot the rocks
at the base of the kelp-trees; even here one is
reminded of the heavens.

These great fields of kelp in the sea, anchored to the rocks with their shell - bound

roots, are useful as well as beautiful, for kelp is washed ashore and hauled away in wagons, to make good manure. Indeed in New England it is counted of such value that rights to take the kelp from certain beaches have been deeded from generation to generation, and lawsuits have sprung from stealing or appropriating kelp. In France the kelp-gatherers cut it at low tide and sell it to the farmers. By and by our coast kelp will not be allowed to wastefully rot on the beach. Sometimes the fishermen who handle the live kelp a great deal in their lobster-trapping become kelp poisoned, which somewhat resembles oak poisoning. Not all are subject to it. Have you ever rowed in the smooth waters of Santa Barbara Bay and examined the beautiful kelp forests?

Be sure the submarine life has its tragedies and its joys, its bitterness and its pleasantries. My fancy sees some slumbering halibut disturbed by the nose of a provoking porpoise. Crawfish, spider crabs, and fiddlers supply the ludicrous in God's submarine creations. Yonder an approaching shark strikes fear into the very bones of a school of slender shrinking fish. Many are the seals who, silently rising, have bitten off a foot of an unsuspecting sea gull, floating quietly outside the surf line. The halibut hides in the sand on the bottom of the ocean, almost invisible; as the little fish come near him, he flaps his great fins, rises up, and seizes in his mouth a whole school of the little fish. And countless teredos are at work, little by little, boring into the spiles of yonder pier, — massiveness being assailed by microbes, as it were. Destruction is not reserved for the earth alone.

It would weary you were I here to enter a complete fish directory of the denizens of our sea. It is enough if I make mention of the savory barracuda, the excellent yellow-tail, and the bonita, or Spanish mackerel, caught by trolling. Four hundred yards offshore is the place to expect the biting to begin. The bonita's favorite food is flying-fish. In Southern Californian seaport towns it is common to hear the glad exclamation, " The yellow-tail are running," and off to the boats the people hasten. The surf-fish is often caught by casting a line from the beach into the surf. Other game of the sea are fine sardines, good sea bass, the peerless graceful sea trout, the delicious croker, the pretty yellow-fin, and the shining smelts. It is pleasant to go out in a dory and make fast to the kelp, tying one of its strands to the bow, and fishing down into the submarine garden below. The great red groupers, belonging to the cod family, are found in two places in Santa Monica Bay, — off Redondo and off Point Duma, in a deep hole, where the lead sinks sixty fathoms. This fish is good to salt, or it makes an excellent chowder. Among the

curiosities of the Pacific hereabout are the marvelous Jewfish, the mottled kelp eels, and the
sharp-toothed red sheephead, which is the delight of Mexicans, and the dislike of Americans.

But in enumerating our fish I must not forget the happy schools of porpoises. See them
out there ! a solid marine mile of them, scam-
pering across the blue sea, seemingly at play.
Their snowy line is ploughing the water into
foaming furrows. Sometimes they come close
in to the beach, and then we can watch them
slowly searching for food. Sometimes they
are visible right in the wall of a breaking wave,
and the effect is the same as when one looks
at the large fish in the aquarium at Brighton,
England. Who will build an aquarium in our
bay ? A porpoise seems to be the essence or
the best synonym of vitality. Its only rival
in vital energy is the humming-bird. What
force they have ! I have seen the old apparently teaching the young to leap and dive and
to find food. In Fisherman's Cove, beyond
Redondo, under the high cliffs, the porpoises
love to disport themselves.

In the Psalms we read that they who go
down to the sea in ships see the wonders of the
Lord in the deep. Let me illustrate by relating a wonder in our own bay. The sharks lay
their eggs here. The yolk, so to speak, can be
seen through the outside. The egg is shaped
like a rectangular purse, with little prongs at

each corner, to which hang quantities of little strings which the mother shark attaches to the kelp by winding them about it (or else they adhere of themselves). On the kelp they suspend until they are hatched. Hundreds of eggs each shark lays, but probably many become food for fishes, porpoises, and seals. Now comes the wonderful protection of Providence, to prevent the extinction of the species; for in color and general appearance the eggs resemble the kelp to which they are attached, so that sharp eyes only could detect them.

It reminds one of the divine care in making the rabbits of Colorado change from brown in summer, the color of the hills, to white in winter, when snow covers the ground. Thus do they escape extinction by the wolf.

After the sharks' eggs are hatched the cases float ashore and are found on the beach curled up and dried.

The spotted leopard shark is common in these waters. Sometimes these sharks play havoc with the fishermen's gill-nets, which are put out in moonlight nights for smelts. Let a leopard full five feet long get in the net, and it means much work the next day to repair the broken meshes. In the seine the sweet-tasting pompano are here caught.

" I won't go out to-day, it is foggy. I can't catch any fish to-day," said the best fisherman on the coast to me. " Why not ? " I said.

"Oh," said he, "fish live in colonies, and to find where they are I have to take my bearings by certain landmarks from the sea, and I could not see the shore to-day from my boat. You see, I know where their colonies are." So the fancy is suggested that fish live in submarine fish cities, and are social in their habits. It may be they have some coöperative protective arrangement or association.

In February, 1894, thousands of dead fish were washed ashore all along the coast, from San Francisco to San Diego, — halibut, barracuda, sharks. They seemed to be in a kind of lethargy. At first people thought the phenomenon was caused by inhaling gases from submarine seismic disturbances, or volcanic eruptions under the sea. Others thought it was a contagious disease, just as murrain spreads among cattle. As to the volcanic-gases idea, do you not remember how, in the "Last Days of Pompeii," after the eruption of Vesuvius the fish came ashore dead? One fisherman told me that the lights of these dead fish were extended as if gaseous fumes had been inhaled. Others unwisely said kelp blossoms and dynamite were at the bottom of the mystery. But I think the general verdict was that this fish plague was caused by worms inside the fish. Some were found whose liver, sides, and back — practically the whole fish — were full of worms.

In May, 1895, thousands of parrot-beaked squid were washed ashore in our bay. Whether these were pursued by a school of large fish and perished in the surf, or whether this occurrence was also caused by disease, I cannot say. At this time there came countless numbers of sea fowl and buzzards to partake of the squid.

On our shores are found the beautiful iridescent abalone shells, out of which jewelry has been made from aboriginal times until now. They vary in size from the very tiny shells, hiding under the rocks, to those measuring perhaps eleven by thirteen inches. The abalone meat is dried and sent to China, where it is a prized food. Narrow, ear-shaped abalones are found on the China coast. It is delightful to go abalone hunting among the rocks.

The scallop also is found on some parts of our coast. This beautiful shell is found on the shores of Palestine also. The pilgrims of long ago used to wear them as a witness that they had visited the Holy Land.

Then we have cockles, which are a popular food product of France also. Never shall I forget my elation when first I found cockles imbedded in the mud under the rocks at low tide. I was reaping without having sowed. How grateful to my palate was the first one eagerly devoured. The liquid of these cockles is even more delicious than clam broth.

There are also clams here, the common kind and the razorback. At the lower-low tide you see men with rakes over their shoulders, or drawing them through the sands to rake up the clams. Visions of a fine steaming Yankee clam chowder make this work light.

Mussels there are besides, that product of the rock-bound coasts which Frenchmen like better than we. The mussel is furnished with a kind of rope which it can attach to a rock or weed to hold the creature in position when the current of the tide is strong. Freshly gathered mussels have weeds fastened to them which, when rubbed in the dark, glow with a brilliant marine phosphorescence. I knew a child who wanted to take some mussels home and "keep them tame."

Very inferior oysters are also found on our rocks. In such places also we have seen great barnacles carrying little barnacles on their backs. Possibly this may have been the object lesson which taught the Indians how to carry papooses. Here, too, the crabs scamper away under shelving ledges, as if for their very life.

In the spring the crabs change their shells, and one finds strewn on the beach a quaint collection of odd forms of their last year's clothes. I have been told by Massachusetts fishermen that a lobster there, during the process of his annual change of shell, is protected against the attacks of his enemies by another

lobster whose shell is still hard. Perhaps the
crabs, too, have such friends.

Some ancient submarines of the hermit-crab
family certainly live for others, because I have
seen scores of barnacles clinging tightly to
their shells, thus securing support, defense, and
locomotion.

SEA LIONS, SEALS, SEA OTTERS, WHALES, AND SEA SERPENTS

A great sea lion lifting his head high out of
the sea is a fine sight.   He is watching, suspi-
ciously, the movements of his observer on the
beach.   See him open his great mouth as if
with a yawn ! His observer is I, and I am
on horseback, taking a three-mile ride on the
beach to Flower Cañon.   After his yawn he
sinks into the sea, and after swimming in the
same direction I am going for some two hundred yards, comes to the surface again, raises
himself higher, and takes a closer look at me.

This programme of scrutiny and submarine
versus beach racing is continued, much to my
amusement ; and, to the credit of the lion be it
said, we cross the line at the cañon at about
the same time.

It is a sad sight to see a dead sea lion washed
up among the rocks, the prey of some man's
cruelty who shot just for the shot, knowing he
could never get him, even if he were hit.

Once in Oregon a man was driving along the

beach in a buggy. He saw a sea lion on the sands. He lassoed the lion, and tying the rope to his carriage axle, started for his home, proud of his conquest. The horse dragged the lion for a while, but, after a little, the lion, objecting to such treatment, concluded to return to the ocean. In spite of all he could do the lion out-pulled the horse, and soon had the buggy half in the surf. With quick presence of mind the man cut the rope, and, it is said, was glad to get home alive. The sea lion's trophy was a rope necklace.

The seals of Southern California are not generally the fur-bearing variety; but a great number of true fur-bearers were once seen at Hueneme. The seals on the Channel Islands are caught with lassoes and then sold to zoölogical gardens, where they are often taught to perform many sagacious acts. In London I have seen one who would sit down in a chair as nicely as you please.

Once we surprised a slumbering seal sunning himself on the sands. I had no club nor firearms, but running up to him as if to take hold of him, I soon changed my mind when he, awakening, drew himself up on his haunches and faced me with opened mouth and a well-preserved set of teeth. I had nothing further to say. With zeal the seal slid down the beach and was away!

When the seals cry or bark it is a sign of

rain, it is said. It cannot be so at the Cliff House rocks near San Francisco, for then the rain would never cease.

The rich sea otter with his costly coat was once a frequent sight in these waters; but now hunted for his fur, that St. Petersburg noblemen may be by him adorned, he is well-nigh extinct. I have seen one family of sea-otters near Point Duma.

Whales can be seen spouting quite often in the bay, and further north on the coast are two whaling stations. Sometimes a dead whale drifts ashore for the seeming especial benefit of the railroad companies, that bring down thousands of people from Los Angeles to see his majesty.

In Monterey there is a walk or approach to the old church made of the vertebræ of whales. Such a vertebra makes a pretty good seat.

Of course the sea serpent visits Southern California. He always does. When I saw him last he was a long, mast-like log with a cross spar nailed on. At a distance and as the swells of the sea bobbed it about, the cross-piece rising out of the water like a long neck and head, I was ready to be certain it was alive, until I found it was not. At another time the sea serpent consisted of a great mass of seaweed, the full length of the deep-water California variety, tightly bound into a sort of rope, which, as it rose and fell on the rolling of the sea, was enough like a serpent to declare that you had seen one, — almost.

FRAGMENTS

When will our people dry their own fish instead of buying it? Sardines abound in our seas, our hills of olives yield oil, but we send our money to France instead of developing that industry. Sardines can be put down in a keg in vinegar and salt for all the year round. The fish are waiting to be caught.

In the Bay of Monterey salmon are caught, but they *very* rarely come into our Southern waters. They are taken by trolling. It is said to be the only place in the world where salmon in the ocean can be taken with hook and line.

Below Monterey is a Chinese fishing village. It is very interesting to visit. I have seen the men home-coming from the sea, and their children would wade into the water to inspect the catch. Soon one of the men threw out a shark on to the beach, and then were the children delighted, gloating over his capture and death. Similar was an Hawaiian scene, when the Kanakas would wade into the water and take the fish from the nets, eating them uncooked and just as they came from the sea.

Vancouver halibut are now taken to Boston on ice. That would have astonished the Puritans. The Pilgrim Fathers would scarcely have thought the halibut supply could ever vanish!

BIRDS OF THE BEACH

But what would the beach be without birds?
And birds there are, as I can bear witness.

Perhaps the most distinctive among the
Southern California sea birds are the pelicans,
or "swans of the sea," — a name well express-
ing their appearance. They sometimes fly with
long-sustained flight just along the surf line,
and barely above the water ; as the wave rises
they rise, and accommodate themselves to the
rise and fall with wonderful ease. When they
do this they are often on long journeys, and
sometimes after surf-fish.

Again, a pelican will dart with amazing velocity from a high flight and dive swiftly after a
fish that is underneath ; a great splash he made
in jumping out of the water, which the pelican
saw with astonishing vision. He seizes the fish
with his long hooked beak under the water,
and, rising to the surface, gulps him down into
his capacious pouch. Sometimes a company of
pelicans will dive together, and afterward float
on the water, chattering, exultant over their
success. But generally speaking, the pelican
is a slow-flying, majestic, dignified bird ; indeed,
when he is full grown, he has earned the title
of "Grandpa Pelican."

On a sunny day you can see them on the
rocks near the shore, expanding and drying their
great outstretched wings. Once we shot a rare

white pelican, a tourist from British Columbia waters, whose tip to tip measurement was eight feet. In the twilight it is amusing to hear the pelicans on the roosting-rocks talk to each other. They evidently compare notes as to what sort of fish are running in the bay.

The pelicans are often accompanied by smaller birds who eat what Sir Pelican does not swallow. He is a grand fisherman, and catches more fish than he can eat. Long live the beneficent pelican! And there is some chance for him, because, fortunately, he himself is not edible.

These birds are our winter guests from the North. People who can afford it, and who need it, — those whose blood is thin from disregard of the laws of health, — imitate the pelicans and seek winter warmth here. Ah! men pay dearly for wealth.

In the spring the pelicans leave us for their resting places, many going to Humboldt Lake in Nevada. At this season large numbers of these birds fly at night over Mount Lowe in their journey northward, as Professor Lowe informs me.

The sea gulls on this coast are beautiful birds. How graceful they are as they float along, their pinions resting on the resisting air! Have you ever seen the gulls flapping hurriedly off the rocks as they see a swell approaching, about to dispute possession of their perch? The shrill cries of the flying hungry gulls are a feature of gull-life, while in bad weather their wild cry sounds above the storm. In the spring when the barley fields are being ploughed up the gulls fly inland several miles to eat the worms in the ground ; an odd sight, and one that always interests strangers, is to see gulls, like blackbirds, following the plough.

When the ducks arrive from the north they are lean after their long flight, but they soon become fat on our fine feed. See that lazy duck as he sits dozing on the wave, lulled to sleep by the gentle wave ; he is contented with Southern California. There are many varieties of duck here. The canvasbacks are found chiefly in inland waters like Bear Valley Lake. The sprig and blue bill make their winter quarters here, and the rare masked-head duck, a visitor from Arctic waters. The great green heads of the mallards, shining in the sun, stir the hunter's heart, and when the birds are brought home they arouse the housewife's skill.

The coots arrive before the ducks. Coots are very stupid birds, which fact has given rise to the expression " stupid as a coot."

Some Eastern people who settled in this country were unaccustomed to the different varieties of sea fowl. Everything that flew like a duck, a duck they counted it, and as such fit to be eaten. Their inexperience brought them trouble. First, in happy expectation, they killed a cartload of coots, only to find them nauseating. Then their courage was restored by the excellence of some fine mallards that they shot. Again, bravely taking to the hunt, mud-hens, sawbills, and wire-tails were killed, only to disappoint the appetite again. They afterwards learned that the natives ate such birds when on the verge of starvation, and at no other time.

The white egret and the bronze sickle-bill ibis are perhaps the most beautiful sea birds that walk our sands. The stately stork, startled by our coming, salutes us with his dismal cronk, and flying seaward alights upon the buoyant kelp.

Of shags there is legion. I have seen the sea-line horizon darkened by their unbroken ranks flying north or south. It is picturesque to see the great rocks at sundown fringed with these piratical-looking birds.

Among the early fall birds to arrive are the pretty bobabouts (we call them). They are small snipe-like birds; they light on the shallow pools by the lagunas, and, revolving quickly, stir up the waters, and then eat the particles which thereupon rise to the surface.

Then, of course, we have the killdeer plover, beloved by other birds because his shrill warning note proclaims some danger. Many a death from gun or hawk has he averted; and he struts as proudly as if he knew his importance.

One of the most remarkable sights by the sea is when a school of large fish pursue a school of small fish to eat them. Then there is a battle royal! From far and near the sea fowl hasten; for their keen eyes have seen the stirred waters. A swarm of gulls, sea pigeons, and pelicans circle about in the air over the struggle in the water, now diving for a crippled sardine or seizing a frightened pompano. Still other birds come to the feast, and countless shags fill up the ranks like battlefield thieves who rob the dead. Winged harpies are they instead of camp-followers.

Now the sun sets on the sea; and all are happy because they are spending the summer at Santa Monica instead of at Redlands.

RANCH LIFE

So you have never before been on a ranch?
I am glad to welcome you to the Rancho
Beautiful, that you may have a glimpse of real
Southern California. I shall delight in your
delight, for to view a country for the first time
îs a great pleasure; and your eyes and ears will
be kept busy with the new wild flowers and the
strange bird-notes.

When first I sought a country home I told
a friend I wished to find a farm near the ocean,
and under the lee of the mountains; with a
trout brook, wild trees, a lake, good soil, and
excellent climate, one not too hot in summer.
To this hope my good wife demurred, saying,
"You ask too much." Such, however, was the
picture of an ideal farm which came to my
mind. But my friend said, "I know such a
place, I think, but I would like to refresh an
old memory and see it again." So he went,
and came back to me, reporting it just as he
had thought, and that it was for sale. Well,
we went to see it; sure enough, there was the
hope realized, the mental picture portrayed in
reality. So we bought it. God, in his goodness, had brought me to just my ideal farm.

I have grown to love this land. When we moved from the city to the country, it seemed like returning from folly to truth. Then did I first grasp the lines

"God made the country, but man the city;"

and Cooper's

"Oh! friendly to the best pursuits of man;
Friendly to thought, to virtue, and to peace,
Domestic life in rural pleasures passed."

Oh! to be free from assailing care; to see no envious faces, no saddened eyes; to see or hear no unkind look or word! To absorb the peace the hills have, to drink in the charm of the brook, and to receive the strength of the mountains, by dwelling in their company, — this is living! To lose one's self by the side of the sea! Free indeed am I! A freeholder! Behold, these hills are mine in trust; none, save my country, disputes my right to yonder ocean; through Christ the sky is mine. Yes, I am a monarch of all I survey; which reminds me how Abraham Lincoln once said of a United States surveyor in California, who obtained large lands after he had surveyed them, that he was monarch of all he surveyed. It *is* a temptation to some, to many indeed, who have obtained much worldly goods, to sit down, and say, "Soul, take thy ease;" yet, in the midst of these temporal blessings and beauties, may I not let myself find therein my chief consolation, since then I should lose the only real consolation, — that which depends upon God through Christ for peace, hope, joy, and a good eternity.

Here in these almost holy hills, in this calm and sweet retreat, protected from the wearing haste of city-life, — here time flies; but only as the farm birds flit from tree to tree, not as the lark speeds pursued by the hawk. The ennobling stillness makes the mind ascend to heaven.

It is delightful to live in such a place that, when the prevailing winds blow, one can send one's mind in the direction whence the wind comes, and realize that it sweeps over a pure expanse of ocean, or over righteous aromatic mountains; and not to be obliged to breathe the air that is blown over an iniquitous city or over some malodorous low-lands. In this good country you need not fear to take a deep, long breath. Surely 't is life to live in this wonderland !

Happy the man to whom Nature has not lost its charm. Unhappy he who, enslaved and engulfed by ambition, mammon, care, or pain, cannot listen to nature and enjoy the sounds of her songs.

> Oh, who would live in a city ?
> Not I, not I.
> Oh, who would live in the country ?
> 'T is I, 't is I.

It stirs many happy thoughts to narrate to you the tale of the halcyon days in which we laid out this landscape, or, rather, added some human touches to what before was divine. Our smiling valley was as a coliseum in the hills, and it appeared, a friend once said, as if the mountains had stepped back to give us space for our home. To enter the valley we made a mile of road. This long roadway was so built along the edge of the foot hills that the little valley was not to be seen until, near its end, the road made a sharp turn, and lo! away down beneath you were the buildings, and orchards, and children, and chickens. Not until long afterward did we learn that we had unconsciously achieved the triumph of the landscape gardener's art, namely, to make the chief beauty of a place appear as a surprise at the end of an avenue.

That fountain we placed before the house with such enthusiasm! Nothing enlivens a little landscape like a joyous fountain. See it splash! See it shoot upward as the pressure varies! A fountain is a very synonym of childish merriment.

Those trees over there? They are wild walnuts. The California native nuts have sweeter, richer, more oily meat than the Eastern shagbark, and are superior in flavor to the English walnut, yet you never see them on sale; Americans have no time to open them, perhaps.

A wild-walnut nutting in our October,
When the merry winds are showering nuts down,
Is a pleasure well known to country folk brown,
While poor pale city people stay under cover.

"What are those trees climbing the air?"
Oh, those are eucalypts. They live, after they
have got a two-year start, without our giving
them water. They have deep tap roots, mois-
ture-seeking: were it not for this, I should be
constrained to say that in summer-time they
must live on the disintegration of their tissues.
There are many varieties of this tree: one, the
ficifolia, has beautiful red blossoms; another
has lemon-scented leaves. They are evergreen.

The eucalyptus and its golden-blossoming
comrade, the grevillia, came from Australia,
you know. It was benignant of that land to
so serve California. They satisfied her one
need. I knew the man who first sent the
eucalyptus seeds to this State from Australia,
and also the man who planted the first grove
of them, — a little forest. The former was that
veteran, Bishop William Taylor.

Suppose we take a walk, pick and eat some
tangerine oranges. They are ripe now. Do
they not taste good? Let us leave the home-
garden roses, fleur-de-lys and sweet alyssum.
Rose-scented air is all right, but after all wild
flowers are the only flowers. Give me the wild
garden. See that field of bright johnny-jump-
ups. This bunch of yellow flowers, with their

green leaves intermingled, is worth a florist's shop window. Smell! "What is that tall stalk crowned with a magnificent white flower?" Oh, that is the Spanish bayonet. Look on the mountain: they stand as sentinels here and there. It is a much sought honor to bring home, on horseback, the first bayonet of the season. Yes, I think you can cut one. Come up through this hillside tangle of chilecota, and glistening red-blossomed gooseberry bush. We will pass through that sumac brush, weaving our way as intricately as yon golden-thread vine makes its way over its neighbors. Ah! Here we are; the prize is yours!

I see by your countenance that you love Southern California already. You are only one more to be added to a long list. This land is as dear to our hearts as is an edelweiss to a Swiss in a foreign land. He keeps it pressed between his Bible's leaves, and thus carries with him his native nation and his nation's God. To what else shall we liken this land? It is as pleasant as it is to be writing a book by an oak fire, when it is raining hard outside. It is as precious to a man as is the land he has cleared with his own hands, or his first-raised ear of corn when he holds it in his grasp. We are as delighted with it as is the boy when he first finds he can whistle and whittle. This country is as good as bread, toasted by the open dining-room fireplace and served hot and

mellow to waiting mouths by mother's hand.
It is as beautiful to the heart's estimation as it
is to a mother to see in her husband the father-
love for her children.

> The sleeping smile of a little child
>   Is a beautiful sight to see,
> And when that child is your own, own child,
>   It is joy untold to thee !

But what similes can we employ to describe
the sad lot of a man who never knew Southern
California ?   His life is as uncomfortable as is
a man's position when impaled upon a barbed-
wire fence; it is as sad as it is when an author,
in the midst of a happy inspiration, perceives
that the oil is failing in his evening lamp.

I shall take you on many trips hereabout.
You must know that we have given our own
names to the places around us, because it was
un-named ground.   That high ridge up there,
from which the view is surpassing, we call the
Wunderschön Vista Ridge.   You smile.   Why
should we not ?   In this polyglot country of
ours, why not have such a title ?   It will appeal
to three nationalities.   And there is no one
word in English that will express what *wunderschön* does in German.   You see we please by
that name the Germans, Mexicans, and Anglo-
Saxons who come to see us.   That building
on the ridge ?   That is the Castle in the Air,
— a place where artists go to sketch and paint.
It is an ideal spot for a Claude Lorraine glass.

Yes, there is much to see here and plenty of room. It is as plenty as the Eastern child found it when he went to visit an uncle on a Kansas ranch. There was no yard inclosed about the house, but to each point of the compass the prairies stretched in unbroken reaches to the horizon. The lad looked about to see what he thought of the place, and then his past city experience prompted him to remark to his uncle, "Well, this is a nice place, but where is your back yard?" The immensity of everything in California soon strikes the Easterner, and, like the lad, he also misses Eastern areas and smaller spaces.

Indeed, friend, there are far distances to go to see all I have in mind to show you. You will soon lose your metropolitan complexion and ere long be taken for a Mexican. Once, traveling up the valley of the Rio Grande, in New Mexico, before the iron horse had plunged into those parts, we were told we could make that night's camp at a Mexican's ranch, at Señor Garcia's. At dusk we came up to the ranch house. In the twilight, I approached a dark-visaged sombrero-man, and in my best Spanish inquired if he were Señor Garcia? "No, sir, my name is Greenwood, from Cincinnati," was the reply in my astounded ears.

We have a cactus in the garden I want to show you. It came from the desert. It is utterly homely and repelling, and yet its large

fragrant pink blossom is of such loveliness that
it excels in beauty even the rainbow rose, or
the bloom of any beautiful flower on the
place. Truly this cactus is as much a paradox
as a frog, of which it is said, "You cannot tell
by the size of a frog how far he can jump."
From its looks you would never dream of its
blossom.

Will you take a walk with me? You may
have your choice. What is your mood? If
ambitious, we will climb those Ehrenbreitstein
heights over there, and just beyond them we
can look down into Cataclysm Chasm, an awful
depth. Or, if you are in quietness of mind, let
us go up the narrow wooded lane to where the
old white adobe cabin stands, and so on around,
by Mocking-bird Valley road, home again. Or,
if you choose the sound of waters, let us invade
the mysteries of the great cañon and get near
that mighty red sandstone cliff, which we call
Crag Noble. You can see it from here. It
surmounts and guards an alcove in the foot-
hills. Leaving that, we can get some trout
above the great balanced rock.

If variety is the spice of scenery as well as
of life, surely this sea-mont country, with its
brooks and fields, its woodlands and mountain-
sides, its beaches and rock shores, and all in a
wonderful climate, offer more variety than any
country ever seen, save Chile, perhaps.

The springtime coloring is unique. The

varying shades of green on the hills, made more prominent by the rocks and ledges visible here and there, help the landscape. Our Father in Heaven must love color, for behold its variety in His creations; and, in the Apocalypse, the glimpses of the Heavenly City abound with mention of various hues. So, in the creation of this earth paradise, God must have entered deeply into the joy of its making and beauty.

Therefore, thus once sang unbidden my happy farmer's heart, as it beheld the ocean and the fields blending their colors: —

> Blue and green, blue and green,
> 'T is the fairest sight ever was seen.
> Green and blue, green and blue,
> Oh, my homestead, *how* I love you !

THE SYCAMORE GROVE

It is such a beautiful day, suppose we go over into the Sycamore Grove, and enjoy the restful presence of the green-leaved trees. Never fear the rippling river; there are good stepping-stones across it. A Southern California river has three experiences every year: we can go over it now on these stones; yet only three months ago a team of horses were nearly drowned in its depths, as they were crossing this very ford; and five months *from* now this lovely river will have disappeared in the sandy gravel, — it will not be dead, but running a goodly subterranean stream, ten feet down. In

Arizona the ancients used, in summer, to build submerged dams from the bed-rock up, thus bringing the water to the top, to be taken out in canals for irrigation.

"Yes, Californian, this *is* a day of days!" It is truly Italian, — a *dolce-far-niente-al-fresco-siesta* day. One ought not to speak English to-day.

It is one of those surpassing days when the temperature of the atmosphere blends with the temperature of the body. At such a time our feelings are harmonious and heavenly. In eternity, I fancy, the ransomed live always in such conditions. Why, to-day the very skies seem to lean towards us in sympathy and love, seeking to help men to be better.

Here we are, safely over on the other side. Let us take the winding road that leads through the knee-deep grasses to the Sycamore Grove : there is bird-land. You can always find music there. In the late afternoon it is pleasant to see the mourning doves, with their shrill-sounding flight, coming to drink at the waters. Hark to the notes of the distant cow-bells up the creek, that reality may meet romance, lest you lose your head and think you are really in paradise.

These green glades ought to make any cow-bells musical, — alfilaria, burr-clover, and fox-tail. You know, in the first good rains the burr-clover seed-balls literally spring to life.

They uncoil themselves, receiving motion from the unwinding of their spiral coils, and thus deliver themselves of the precious seeds they contain. Blessed is burr-clover to every one except the cloth-maker, to whom it is a trial to extricate its spines from the cloth you wear. The grazing sheep loves the burr-clover, and after having dined off it he lies down on his dried-clover bed ; but when he arises from his nap, you can see countless burrs sticking to his wool, to remain there until it is removed by carbonization, in a New England mill.

I am glad you brought the gun. We are sure to see quail. We catch a sight of a cotton-tail rabbit, and away he is gone in the brush. Listen ! hear the calling of the quail : they are over yonder. We will get our breakfast by and by.

Sometimes in the morning the voice of a linnet announcing the dawn of day will open my eyes. " Awake ! awake ! " he gently sings, for the time to work has come. Then, anon, our home-quail covey, that we never shoot, come around the early door to find the children's crumbs, and I hear them from my room, " Chirp – chirp ! "

The linnets and the quail, how we love them ! In the spring some one comes in and says, " The linnets are back again ! " Then we enter into their little lives, and mourn with them, when later the wicked racer snakes climb up the

arbor, and rob their nests in the trellis-vines.
Ah! the sorrow from the snakes. Bird tragedies! It is a wonder they sing so much.

Here we are in the heart of the sycamores.
Do you note the formation of this group of
majestic trees? It is like the nave of a cathe-
dral. We call it the Temple, since the woods
were God's first church. See how the glorious white-barked sycamore limbs, covered with
their great green shady leaves, arch over the
aisles, with openings to the blue heavens here
and there to increase our faith. What a place
for an æolian organ!

A hundred yards yonder, in that mass of
leafy shade of sycamores, lies the Isle of Peace.
When you want to be alone go over there, if
the birds' talk won't interrupt your thoughts.
The river breaks and runs all around it, but
you can get over on stones. You will find
strangely hued orioles there. Like movable
jewels set in the air, their flight will catch your
eye. Once a pair of these built on the ridgepole of a rarely used tent we had pitched, and
actually hatched out a brood. You will see
gentle wrens, — they always make me think of
home; and when, like Tityrus, you recline
under the wide-spreading shade, you can watch
a battle in the air, as the little birds pursue
and fight the robber ravens. There lives over
there, also, a family of black flycatchers, with
their jaunty caps, although most of their tribe,

as the linnets, like to be near people and build about the porch or trellis. These little fly-catchers are sometimes seen hovering at the window-pane, trying to capture a fly on the other side of the glass.

The swallows will let you study them. How delicately they skim over the water, sipping as they fly! Nothing is so delicate save a smilax blossom or the soft step of a fawn.

Ah! but these swallows do us much mischief. In the spring they come by thousands on a single day. Before the house the air is alive with their graceful curvèd flights, they seem so glad to reach their chosen resting-place. Alas! what do you think? They soon begin to bring mud from the riverbank, and bespatter our house and windows with it. They ought to go to the cliffs over there and build as God gave them instinct. They used to before we built our home.

So when they assailed our house in myriad numbers then began the battle of the swallows. Again and again did we drive them away with shotguns and demolish their nests plastered against the eaves, but just as often did they return, loath to surrender their selected site; until finally, discouraged by sheets hung out from the windows flapping in their faces, they took to the cliffs and there abode.

The most singular part of it is they come back every year, and have to be driven away.

If you tire of birds you can hunt in the arroyo seco for agates; some are beautiful, almost rubies and emeralds. If you go to sleep instead, look out you do not lie down over a tarantula's nest. You have seen in museums those great, hairy, black spiders, whose venom is only equaled by the rattlesnakes. I think you will not be molested. When we go home, I will show you one of their clay nests. The hinge of the trap-door of their cell is one of God's wonders and California's mysteries. The poison of this beast, for such is he, is so virulent that whiskey has been honored by the title of tarantula juice.

Looking out of our window, at suppertime, I once spied a tarantula crossing a flower-bed in the garden. In a moment I had my stick, and in another, my stick had the tarantula. Three others have we killed. They like to come out at twilight.

Their building skill is indeed wonderful. In Europe, when you meet her educated people, they ask an American first about Niagara, then Yosemite and the Big Trees, and then about the Yellowstone and Old Faithful, the geyser. But there are marvels in our animal kingdom, like the tarantula's nest, that would astonish Pliny.

"What is that noise?" Oh, that is a yellow-hammer driving his beak into a tree; thud – thud – thud. Swift-winged is he and a great housebreaker. They entered my office attic, the rascals. They bore holes through the redwood boards. Insurance policies should be made out in this country against their depredations. Once a yellowhammer, in his abnormal inquisitiveness, crept over the top of my open chamber window, and, stupid! could not get out. I caught the intruder and took him to the children, still in bed, greatly to their delight and his terror.

You know the woodpeckers, their cousins, have a great trick in our high mountains. They drill holes in the pine-trees, circle after circle around the pine, and in these holes stick acorns. What for, do you think? Well, by and by, in some way a worm comes in the acorn, and it is to get that worm this contriving bird goes to all that labor! It must be considered a rare dish, — I suppose his bluepoints or terrapin.

The day is growing old. Ah! I thought it was time for the mocking-birds. Hear that! Talk about music! It is a happy day when the mocking-bird makes his home near your dwelling. Then his woodland solo fills the air morn and eve. One used to imitate a private patented whistle call by which I greeted my wife. In the Mexican language the mocking-bird is called the bird of four hundred tongues.

Yes, we do have robins, once in a great while.

I remember how happy we were when one day we saw two real Yankee robins. It was a welcome sight to a transplanted New Englander.

Let us search this tree for nests. Is not the tree lovely? If I were a bird I would build in an elderberry-tree. Look sharp for a humming-bird's nest. I just saw the proprietor, whose breast so glowed that it would shame a ruby from Ceylon. Besides, the doleful mourning doves build here.

I have only one ungranted wish this day of delight, and that is that I might show you Southern California's *rara avis*, the phaïno-pepla, that magnificent crested, glossy black aristocrat. He is hard to find, but some day we may see him.

I suppose by this time you think, comrade, I know nothing except birds. Well, so be it; but it is pleasant to have something to study besides your old Boston English sparrows. It is such a relief to find a place where the English sparrow has not penetrated. His ubiquitous self, like the Anglo-Saxon race, has been born to conquer. If it keeps on, these invading birds will take our country and give it to the queen. They have not reached our woods yet, but alas! for how long?

Now let us go for the quail. Is your gun loaded?

RANCH THOUGHTS AND MODERN MEMORIES

What hope there is in new ploughed land! Tom and Prince, their great muscles straining to the task, plod steadily along, while the shining ploughshare turns up the sweet-smelling soil. See the blackbirds follow, like porpoises in the wake of a ship : surely the plough is the blackbird's friend. When the last furrow is finished the farmer's heart rejoices, and as he sows the seed, the click of the corn-planter is heard in the land. Now and then he sings to his own tune, —

> " One for the blackbird, one for the crow,
> One for the cut-worm, and two to grow."

A little time is left before dinner : he takes the ruthless hoe and starts in to clear a piece of land of nettles, and proves his good character by not getting angry. No one knows the meaning of the expression "on nettles," unless he has felt them in his hands.

But what is that ? Dinne-r-r-r ! and how glad is he to find on the shady porch an earthen jar, or olla, of cool water to brighten him up. Who could not compose a bit of verse in its honor ?

THE SONG OF THE OLLA

> I sing of the olla, full of water so cool,
> On the porch, under tree or placed in the school.
> The old oaken bucket has a rival now found
> In the hearts of the people who here till the ground.

In distant New England the well-sweep holds sway,
But California people have a different way.
From the spring, or the brook, or the well, if you will,
At evening the housewife earthen ollas does fill.
In these boons to mankind, allowed to remain over night,
While a law in the mean time works its wonder of might,
The water by morning is as cold as if ice
From Tahoe had made it especially nice:
And the coolness still keeps through the heat of the day,
Be it time of the fruitage or harvest of hay.

So I sing of the olla with water so cool;
'T is only fulfilling the good Golden Rule.
Then speed to the olla with feet winged by thirst,
And drink of its water, thanking God for it, first.

How proud we were when we sat down to
dinner at a well supplied table, and realized
that all on the board came from *our* own farm!
We sat up very straight and buttoned up our
coats.   Dinner is the farmer's restful meal.
Sometimes breakfast is perforce so early, in
order to catch the winter morning train, that
we involuntarily used to ask ourselves, "What
is it, yesterday or to-day?"

The afternoon's work in the orchard is pleasant work; trees show such gratitude in growth
for the care you give them.   How happy is a
man when his new orchard is all set out!   What
a relief in its completion!   The birds fly about,
perching upon the tops of the little trees, as if
they thought the orchard was set out for them.
And, by and by, how delighted is the young
orchardist when his trees have grown large
enough to make a considerable shadow.   What

fine trees they are! How he welcomes the
buds; what promises of fruitage! Aye, happiness can be found in the orchard as well as in
the dictionary.

> The breezes that blew seemed to blow for me,
> As I hoed the orchard from tree to tree.
> Oh! I was so happy then.

In Southern California "when our ship comes
in" is changed to "when our orange orchard
comes in bearing;" then, to be sure, we can
afford an organ, and we will go to the beach!
Enough castles in the air have been thus built
in the name of orange and lemon groves to
cover the continent.

By the way, the Spanish way of securing
finely flavored fruits or grapes is to remove
much of the fruit that comes, so that the
strength of the sap goes into just a few
peaches or bunches of muscats.

There is poetry in farming. There is pure
enjoyment. What thrills of joy has the farmer
when he first hears the melody of his own mow-
ing-machine! The waving fields of glistening
grain, when the breezes are chasing and trying
to overtake each other across the waving tops of
the bending barley, the sheen of the barley-blue
sticks showing underneath (what a color is barley-blue!), make up for the tiredness of plough-
ing-time. But alas for the blackbirds that build
in the barley! Behold the blue eggs in the
laborious nest, and here comes the relentless

mower. With its sharp knives the heart-strings of the mother-bird are cut as truly as the grain. Down fall the barley pillars that held up their house, and, uttering shrill cries, the parents hover over the death of their hopes. But we did not tell them to build there.

The smell of the new-mown meadow sends its fragrance over the fields.

Oh, yes, farm life here has many delights; for instance, we have ripe fresh fruits of one kind or another from New Year's to Christmas. If it is not oranges it is figs, and if the figs are gone, it is something else, — something ripe on the trees all the year round.

The following story is a common classic on the Pacific coast. Oft has it been told around the hearth. It illustrates how one farmer succeeds while another fails.

There were two farmers whose farms of equal acres of the same quality joined. Each strong farmer had the same number of strong sons. The first made a great success of farming. The second did not do well; so he said to the first, "Why is it, neighbor, that under equal conditions you succeed and I fail?" "Well," said his neighbor, "in my work I say, 'Come on, boys,' while you say 'Go, boys.'"

It is getting dark on the ranch. A heavy fog is setting in from the sea. Do you notice what a muffled sound the surf has? At regular intervals we hear the dismal sound of the steam fog-signals from the great steamer passing up the coast. They sound like the moanings of a Leviathan.

Now another sound is heard. Our lodge-gate bell is a mile away, at the entrance gate. It always announces the coming of friends or foes. It is a singular bell; it is nothing more nor less than the barking of the dogs the herder keeps at the cabin by the gate. To be poetical we call the shanty our lodge, though it has no ivy nor lattice windows.

Again the dogs! Methinks their barking bespeaks some traveler belated.

How pleasantly secure one feels who, while lying abed, hears the watch-dogs outside barking vociferously, threatening the coyotes or pumas, robbers or tramps. Now the sharp falsetto of the collie sounds the alarm, and then comes the deep bass growl and Myron-Whitney-like tones of our great Saint Bernard as he barks out his "beware, beware."

A FARMER'S FANCIES

During the long winter rains, when the swollen rivers rush fiercely to the sea, and the rain seems likely to fall forever, how often in fear should we wonder if disaster were not coming, were it not for the rainbow promise of God.

Hear the gutters sing! See the leaden rain-bags, wind-driven, float across the valley, until, through pressure, they break, and their contents pour down in harvest-assuring showers. It is a goodly, benignant rain, in such sheets of showers. See the trees toss their heads in the wind !

After the first rains in Southern California the dust of the dry season is washed out of the air, and the charm of the atmosphere is remarkable. The mountains then become twice as beautiful and the sea thrice as blue. How good God is to make the fields all green again !

But the storm is not over, for, look ! the clouds are still clinging to the mountains. Yet really I am not sure, the weather is so unreliable. I lost my faith in it the other day because my friend, who was my chief admiration as a weather prophet, was himself deceived. Thus it was : —

It was on the third day of December. We met on the road, my said neighbor and I. The all important question, " When do you expect rain ? " brought forth the following reply : " Well, I am sure this is going to be another dry year. I have reasons for knowing, as I have for years observed the game, and know their habits when a dry year is upon them. I am able, thus, to feel certain we shall have but little rain this year." He spoke under a cloudless sky. Yet, would you believe it, in two days' time there began to fall from heaven such copious showers that the rivers roared, and the roads were washed out, and my poor friend caught la grippe before he got home from his trip outside after lumber. No, reader, the weather and mines are two subjects we should be careful about.

One beneficent phenomenon of Southern California, which I think statistics will prove, is the frequency with which it rains in the night, while the sun shines the next morning. It clears in the night. When I first came here to live, a Californian in the Pullman said I should find it so. I did not believe him. I thought he was trying to sell me some land. But you can believe me.

Were it not for the rain, our cattle would die; so, in literature, cattle should be mentioned after the rain.

Cattle on the mesas, sheep on the hills, goats on the mountains in California. When you do not have a dry year, and when murrain passes you by, cattle-raising is a happy life. His grazing herds on the hills around, a man can imagine Abraham's life.

How proud was I when the blacksmith made my first branding-iron! What a fine triangle that surely is! To get in the saddle and ride through the herds and think how much that steer will weigh next May, and to watch him grow, — that is pleasant. With what pride does a farmer view his fattened three-year-old steer! How he needs and wants his value in money, and yet from association's sake he can hardly bear to see him go out of his gate to the abattoir. Has he not seen him come up from a small calf, toddling against his mother, until he little by little got heavier and heavier, and now he is the pride of the fields? Few possessions become so much esteemed.

When the farmer sleeps, his young cattle are growing; such is a happy waking thought. After breakfast, he goes out and sees the browsing kine with curling tongues gathering the tender moist morning grasses into their mouths, and he salutes the pleasant-visaged cows by name. One he calls Brin, another Brindle, still another Bryn Mawr; but this he never says when any one is about.

It is interesting to know the ways of cattle, — to see their feeling when one dies of fever or some other sickness; they will stand about as if in real sorrow. Again, in the cold wet rains I have seen them standing close together, their sides touching, thus proving an animal-mutual-benefit association. As grazing cattle avoid the windward side of a hill, so should men avoid those places and persons that incite them to sin, and those conditions which jeopardize their health.

One evening among the men there were whispers of cattle thieves. Blood had been found on the trail. A man had told another that he had deer meat in the gunny-sack on his saddle. *He* could not shoot a deer; it was a calf, we all thought. When a man wants to know if he can forgive an enemy, let him put the grace in his soul to the test of forgiving a cattle-thief. If he can pardon that, he is a good man. Just think of raising a steer up to be a three-year-old, and then losing him in a night!

It is a fair sight to see a large untouched pasture, whose grasses have been allowed to come to maturity, undisturbed. We have just turned our zoölogical collection into it. That is the children's donkey: his name is Don Quixote — Don-key-o-ti, don't you see? He is a remarkable burro; he will lie down and roll under a barbed-wire fence. Our lambs, Angora kids, pigs, poultry, and the Roman peacock are all enjoying the field. Do not you think in case of a famine our place would be a good one to come to? Pigs are not altogether disagreeable, if they are black and have plenty of range: I am sure those three over there, Breakfast, Dinner, and Supper, are pleasant to behold. How they must wonder what the garbage pail contains, when they see the boy coming with their *dejeuner à la fourchette!*

It is said, by the way, that pigs cannot swim without cutting their throats. It is not so. Mine can; although in swimming long distances their long horny hoof-toes might cut gashes in their necks.

Pretty sights are to be seen on a farm.

What? Why, a fleet of little ducks stemming the up-current of their home river. Alas! that those evil crows should have once killed fifteen of ours. Then the corral full of white Angora kids, — their whiteness made all the whiter by the presence of the little fellow all chocolate color, — three hundred of them; it looks like a field of snow. How they play! They see-saw on that plank the herder has fixed for them. The young goats are excellent eating, as the Israelites well thought.

But goat-meat is not good when you buy a leg of mutton, and, bringing it home, find the long goat hairs on the meat, and ejaculate, miserable, "Why, it is goat!"

In the time of Moses the people were wise enough to stew the goat meat. It was against the law to stew a kid in its mother's milk, which was probably a statute to curb the cruelty of the people, and to make their minds gentle.

Leonardo, our goat-herder, had a remarkable financial experience. Several years before he had borrowed a dollar from a friend, who came one day for his money. They conversed, and it seemed right to both that interest should be paid. Neither could compute it, nor had either any idea what amount to charge or pay. They settled on a five-dollar basis, one for principal and four for interest. Has civilization been of use to Leonardo? Yes, indeed, but his grandfather never would have thought of paying interest save by some kindness in return, if a chance occurred.

Mountaineer, our fine dapple-gray horse, had a sad fate. Driven down the beach too rapidly for so heavy a horse he was prostrated with colic. He fell in the surf, and with difficulty Olof removed the harness, got the spring wagon backed away, and, mounting his mate, rode rapidly for help to the vaquero with his riata. Coming up, the vaquero soon lassoed poor Mountaineer, and on horseback drew him out of the surf. But it was too late ; he was then almost drowned. We worked over him a long time, but in vain. He is buried by the side of the loud-sounding sea.

It would not be fair to leave the bees out of this book, — their hives are found on so many of our ranches. It is pleasant to consider how the bees are working every day for you without ceasing, and that the food they are making comes from the flowers.

> My bees are making honey for me
> As they fly from flower, shrub, and tree.

And what patience and industry they have ! Go to the ant and the bee, thou sluggard ! Sir John Lubbock states that a single bee with all its labors will not collect more than a teaspoon-ful of honey during a season.

Here in this southland you can buy honey made from orange blossoms or from the wild white sage.

> But the best honey of all, it seems to me,
> Is what you find wild in a sycamore-tree.

The finding of a bee tree is a great occasion. In a hollow in its trunk, away up high sometimes, is the bees' treasure house, where for months they have been storing away their precious honey. Ah! just look in there! there is spreading for a thousand slices of mother's bread.

> If you think you're as young as you used to be
> Just try to climb a spreading sycamore-tree.

Two Scotchmen in the early days, I have read, came to California. Each wished to bring with him some memorial of his homeland. One brought the thistle, his country's emblem; the other a small swarm of honey-bees. Those men have passed away; one brought with him a curse to our land, the Scotch thistle; while the other brought a blessing, for the bees increased and filled the mountains. And the account I quote from added, "Which do you bring when you move into a new locality, — good or evil?"

I have some fine thistles that would cause a wandering Scotchman to rejoice at the sight, but if he owned the land he would prefer the goldenrod.

Bees and orchards do not work together well. One hive may do no great harm if you have a large wild range. Sometimes a bee ranch in an orchard neighborhood will ruin the latter business, for the bees eat the fruit.

The yellow-jackets are a great trial to us. The rascals just live off our apricots. A friend of mine said the only way to prevent this pest and have enough peaches to eat, was to plant more trees than the yellow-jackets could possibly eat the fruit of.

No, it is not all sunshine in Southern California. The gophers and the chicken hawks have declared war against us : there is no hope of arbitration. So we lay in a supply of ammunition : strychnined raisins and carrots, traps and guns. The present state of the war is favorable — to us.

Ah! we have paid in these years a heavy tribute of poultry to the denizens of the air and brush. Many a good breakfast has been loss to us and gain to the coyote, hawk, or owl. And, alas! our vegetable kingdom also has had to pay large taxes to those patience-destroying gophers. One could forgive a gopher for eating just a little, but when he puts in his little pocket a good lot more, and runs off with it into his hole, it is disgraceful.

But we have made an alliance with experience and hope for victories in the future.

Weeds play their part in the drama of Southern California life. Who among us has not met in battle the tumbleweed, which, when ripe, is a great ball-shaped mass, and becomes the plaything of the autumn Santa Annas? and the loco-weeds, which kill your sheep after

making them *non compos mentis*? and the chile-
cota vines that want to monopolize the earth?
and the persistent nettles? and— Yes, we do
have pusley here.

These are not all of our troubles. We have
mosquitoes, but they are not half so venomous
as those in New Jersey, nor so numerous. Then
there are fleas, too.

The scale also wars against the orchardist,
but science and the lady-bugs are driving away
that terror.

I want this to be "a plain unvarnished tale,"
so I must say that we have other troubles, such
as water-rights, jumping claims, live-stock preferring your own grass to their owners' (although
the latter may know something about this), and,
rarely, dry years.

Last evening a mountain lion was troubling
the night. The dogs barked till daybreak. The
puma's shrill screams made the young stock
nervous, and men clutched their rifles.

I have just seen the lion's great tracks in
the soft ground.

THE RODEO

"Bonifacio, we shall have the spring rodeo on
the twentieth of March," called out the owner of
the rancho to a passing horseman.

"Then, seguro, I will be there; many thanks."

Seguro is a wonderful word, and gives great
weight to a Mexican's statement when spoken

in an earnest tone, provided the eye of the
speaker looks sincere.

"Segurro, I will be there."

The twentieth is here. Early in the morning some fifteen mounted men assemble at the
ranch-house and, starting forth, hunt the hills
and valleys in a twenty-mile area for cattle, and
drive them all to a certain vale, where there
is a large sycamore-log corral.

The patron, or owner, in the morning tells
each man which course to take, for, as the
range is so many miles in extent, like a general he must place his men that no portion be
left unsearched.

"Si, señor, si, señor!" and away they all
go, happy as larks, for it is *the* day of the year.
Not too fast at first, for the vaquero knows
his horse: on his favorite, he rides forth at the
pace of an Indian trot. He thus conquers distances, when Eastern riders would be left behind, trusting to walk and canter diversified.

Oh, the happy vaquero! Who would be a
banker, when he could ride the smiling hills and
hide himself and horse in the tall mustard!
Who would be a slave to desk and electric-
light darkness in a back room, when sunshine
is free to all? Aye, a liberal competence is
splendid, but slavery is often its price.

But then we cannot all be vaqueros.

When the sun has well warmed the hills, the
cattle can be seen approaching the zuma corral

from every direction towards the appointed place. They are all driven together in a great band and halted on a level plain. Then the men ride in and cut out the cows that have calves, which are now about to be branded.

Some men guard the group of cattle so segregated; others hold in check the original herd. When all the calves have been segregated with their mothers, then the drive to the corral begins, and amid much shouting, forcing with flying rawhides, and vociferating, they are made to enter the corral; the bars of sycamore are put up, the fire is lighted to heat the brands, and the knife-men sharpen their knives on the oil-stone.

The mothers, remembering their last year's experience, keep their calves close to them, giving a kind of a moaning moo, and licking them with their tongues.

The vaqueros re-cinch their horses and uncoil their riatas. At a word from the owner the lassoing commences.

Then Bonifacio Cosio, with a well aimed cast, captures a strong calf by the head, and in a moment Pasqual curls his riata around the hind legs of the same calf. Both vaqueros then spur their horses in opposite directions and the calf falls to the ground, ready to be treated.

Then up runs Francisco Ruiz with his knife, does the work required, cutting the ear with the patron's ear-mark, and Olof is on hand with the hot brand. Siss-s-s-s! and a fine triangle is left on the buttock of the struggling calf. The calf bawls out his wrath. It is not so painful as it reads.

Meanwhile other riatas have been flying for their prey. There are six horsemen in the great corral. Soon the Nicholson boys, bro-thers, have shown their American skill, and, turning in laughter to the Mexicans, call out, " Aha! see what dos gringos can do!"

The horsemen make it lively for the knife-men and the branders. The wingéd riatas cut the air, and stirring shouts of "Vivo!" "Vivo!" "Hâhle!" "Hâhle!!" "Hâhlele!!!" (spelled phonetically) make the corral ring. All these quick sounds are mingled with the bawling of the cows amid the pain-and-fright cries of the calves.

" The knife! the knife!" "Some salt for this fox-tail-pierced eye!" (Fox-tail is a dried sharp grass-head.) "The brand! the brand!" "El fiero!" "Look out for the taurito!!" "Bring the medicine here quickly!" Such are the sounds.

Sometimes the riata misses its mark, and the vaquero hangs his head in shame. Now he makes a great lass', and pride suffuses his face; although he tries to look unconscious, his at-tempt is a signal failure. "Bravo! Bravo!"

Then the patron or his major-domo calls out " Fix the saddles," and all dismount, and so do, re-cinching. The knife-men wipe their wet foreheads with red handkerchiefs, and sharpen their knives. Everybody drinks of the water just outside the corral under the tree, and soon the vaqueros have remounted, ready for work again.

Anew fly the riatas, again and again come the "vivos" and the "bravos," until the vaqueros search in vain for a calf that has not been branded.

The ends of the ears cut off had all been thrown into a box, and are now counted. " How many, Francisco ? " " Tres cientos quinze, señor," that is, Three hundred and fifteen, sir. " Muy bien," says the patron, as he enters the date and number in his stock book. He himself had already counted the calves as they were cut out of the whole herd.

On the corral sides were perched the neighbors, watching, and criticising the points of the cattle. Here, too, were several disappointed lasso-men, for whom there was not room in the corral.

When all is over a bite is taken under the broad branches of a sycamore, and then for the ride home over the rich green hills ! With hanging heads the wearied horses homeward go ; but the vaqueros' tongues fly as fast as their riatas an hour ago.

Many are the tales told that night around the ranch-house fire.

IN OUR CAÑONS

Southern California is not so well watered as Minnesota and Massachusetts. Its water-power is limited: its rivers and brooks are comparatively few, so that wherever water-courses are found in this land they are especially esteemed. The gorges in the mountains, through which flow the brooks and streams, are called cañons, or canyons; and the name "cañon" never falls upon a Californian's ear without causing thoughts of happy days in summer-time.

The loveliest place, to my mind, is a wooded cañon which opens to the sea, offering the crystal waters of its limpid brook as a libation to the spirit of the ocean; an offering brought from the high mountains, which near by gaze downward with wonder at the ocean's vastness; while the sea looks upward in admiration of the sierra's heights. In such a cañon as this did Alessandro and Ramona encamp in their flight.

There are only a few miles on our Atlantic seaboard where the mountains come to meet the ocean, but in Southern California, seacoast and mountain resorts are attainable in one and the same locality.

These cañons that open to the beach have
a large population of trees, flowers, and birds.
Broad-branching sycamores spread their shade
over dozing flocks; their bright green leaves
are fresh-looking when the summer fields are
dry and brown, — a beneficent providence. The
sycamore was the tree of Zaccheus. Do you
remember the odd smell of its leaves? And
how in the arroyo the roots of the great sycamores hold boulders in their tight grasp, growing all about them ? In California cañons and
on hillsides is found the poison oak, which is in
the West a scourge to a delicate skin, as is the
poison ivy in the East. The purpose of this
scrub is a mystery: so are mosquitoes. Do
the following verses solve one mystery ?

POISON OAK

About six thousand years ago —
You need not wonder how I know —
Two oak-trees, living side by side,
Near the mountains, afar the tide,
Suffered abuse from a young oak,
Who disrespect and scoffing spoke.
They reprimanded all in vain ;
Patience was practiced by the twain,
Until from heaven a Voice there came,
And called the forest lad by name :
" For thy neglect of Heaven's laws
Vouchsafed to men and trees because
'T is right and truly ordered so,
Henceforth thou shalt no greater grow ;
Thou, nor thy progeny below,
The noble oaks, thy family ;
And thou shall be a disgraced tree,
And poison-oak thy name will be."

Then the cañons possess beautiful black alders, cottonwoods, and the sweet bay tree. How happy were we when we first found some native maples, real maples! But the live-oak is *the* tree *par excellence*. One great oak in Ramirez Cañon, of massive size and great gnarled trunk, we call Abraham's Oak, in remembrance of the ancient oak in Palestine of the same name, so called because it was thought to have lived in Abraham's day. Its finely colored drab limbs are in pleasing contrast to its depth of green. Many a time have I wished that grand old oak to make me his confidant and reveal the secrets of the past. How many generations of aborigines hast thou fed with thy acorns, oak? Still falls thy fruitage, the food of the past, unappreciated by the present. And when in bloom what a fair sight is a live-oak tree. Sometimes these oaks are in groups, beautifully placed. In Soston Cañon about twenty-five young oaks are growing close together, and their tops blending in foliage make a great umbrella-shaped roof, a fine house. The birds love these trees. In Trancos Cañon I know a noble oak whose boughs almost reach the ground, and on all the branches, even to the lower ones, within your reach, are scores of nests. It is really a compound bird-nursery. Such a chatting of blackbirds when they are worrying over their children having to go out to meet the world!

As for flowers, the most typical are the great

wild tiger-lilies, with stalks five feet high, which grow at the brookside, near by where the miner's lettuce shows its delicate green. The exquisite foliage of the wild gooseberry, and the columbine's red bloom, beautify the slopes, scattered amidst the evergreen sumac. Now and then one finds the chile-cojote or mock-orange, with its yellow fruit; while overhead in the cañon's shady dells you can see that pretty vine, the mountain fringe, with its feathery blossoms draping the trees. Clinging to the trees you see the mistletoe, furnishing us with nature's illustration of retribution; the mistletoe kills the tree, and then has to die itself. Close by, a chile-cota, with its mammoth bulbous roots, runs at will over the underbrush, its spiked seed-balls hanging like fruit, which, by and by, when ripe and dry, will furnish padding to many a bird's nest; for inside the pod there is a fine silky material.

Bird-life abounds here. The great owls here abide. Here Sir Kingfisher watches for his minnow and trout, catching more than the angler; just as the mountain lion kills more deer than the hunter. This is the home of the humming-birds. It seems hard to believe that the humming-bird was not known in Europe till Cortes found it in Mexico. Yet so they say. Its habitat is from Alaska to Tierra del Fuego.

Once I found the rare nest of a titmouse in

Rustic Cañon. *He* is a tailor indeed. But the top-knot California quail is our greatest delight. Hark! a covey is coming to drink! Hide behind this brush. Hear the whirring of their flight, — music to the hunter's ear. Their call is a welcome sound to a hungry camper. Americans say their call says "Bob White! Bob White!" but in Germany the children say the quail thus say, "Fear God, Love God." So leave the city next summer and come to hear the calling of the quail; come and hear the brook sing, and smell the fragrance of the wild shrubs; listen to the rustling of the ripened grain and the chorus of the larks.

A brook has a soothing influence; the music of a riffle is good to put one to sleep. A loud-voiced bee goes buzzing by and awakes your drooping lids. A lazy tortoise slides off his rock into the little pool. Curiosity makes you wide awake; your eyes follow his course in the translucent waters, and now, close by the brook edge, you study the secrets of this little inland sea. Do you notice that great light-green beetle under water? I call him the dog beetle, because with his forefeet he paws his way downward into the sand, and with his hind feet, wonderful to relate, kicks backward the sand pawed up by his forefeet. See him now!

> Yes, the cañon is alive with life,
> There were butterflies about me,
> Blithe birds sang in the bowers,

> And insects, as an army,
>   Were foraging the flowers.

> The brook has made more poets sing
>   Than almost any other thing.

In this coastland many brooks to-day are
wending their way to the sea, smiling, happy,
breaking into laughter as they reach the riffles.
The trees are bending over them with looks of
love, for without the brook the tree would die.
The brookside grasses are nodding good-by as
it goes along, for they, too, live by its moisture.
In its ceaseless journey it ever onward goes, its
mission is never stopped ; it is continually doing
good to the trees and flowers, and kindly carrying a drink to the deep, — a good lesson to me.

I have not called our brooks by name, but
one is so beautiful I should refer to it : —

> The brook La Chusa with its waters sweet,
>   And brookside paths for eager feet,
> Implants in ev'ry weary city heart
>   Freedom from care and tiresome art.

In these cañons the bandits of the early days
made their camps, and here hid to evade capture. At last, driven by losses and desperation,
the Mexicans trailed the bandit Nicolas to his
mountain fastness ; and I know the precipice
over which he leaped rather than be taken alive.
In the upper part of Las Tunias Cañon the in-
famous robber Vasquez made his headquarters.

It was in one of these cañons that we found
the Grotto Beautiful, where the stalactites hang

down in picturesque beauty. The lime forma-
tions make an arch above your head, while
through the opening you look out upon the
blue sky and the green foliage of a sycamore.
In July the whole roof of the grotto is ablaze
with a mass of bright yellow flowers. The
water trickles down through the limestone, and
in the hottest of days coolness can be found.
It is a steep descent to the grotto, but the
sight is one of great variety and beauty. Near
by is an ancient natural cave, used by Indians,
on the walls of which are Indians' red-painted
designs, antlered deer-heads, a disk, and many
odd characters, which may be their sign-words
or may be copies of old Spanish cattle or horse
brands. Not far away is a great boulder, in
which holes were made by the Indians to pound
their acorns in.

Mineral springs are a feature of this neighborhood, and far up in the west fork of the
Sequit, near the headwaters, is a lovely waterfall with a great mass of maidenhair fern fifteen
feet wide, over which the water trickles.

If we follow the course of the stream upward, we pass many spots where we must tarry
awhile; to look into the shaded pools, trout
homes, watching the fish dart under the shelving rocks; or to examine the lovely fern-banks
on the side of the cañon where the sun rarely
shines; to study some stalagmitic accretions, or
to laugh at a gray squirrel as he gracefully

jumps, or flies almost, from tree to tree.   Now,
wondering at the cañon's towering walls, we
find ourselves far up in the heart of the coast
range where the brook was born.   The moun-
tain-sides come close together, leaving barely
room for the streamlet to run.

Up here the water seems sweeter to the
taste.   How many places there are that invite
one to stop and drink!   See that miniature
waterfall!   If we stand on some rocks in the
brook below it, our chest rests against the flat
boulder over which the fall leaps, and our lips
are just in place to drink from the pool above.

By and by in our winding way we see another
pool we cannot pass, so, bending low, I drink
from my woodland chalice, the brooklet; it is
studded and jeweled with bright agates and
stones of various colors.   To slake my thirst
the mountain water runs down into my mouth.
And such water! flavored by ferns, by water
grasses, and aromatic roots, just enough of
every ingredient, God's own distillation!

How oft on summer days have I gone to a
certain spring, unknown to others, and restored
my energy and endurance.   The wild flowers
grow by its gracious banks and drop their
ripened honey into it to make it sweet.   Sweetwater, I call the spring, and of it he who drinks
would drink again.   Indeed, I think so much of
this spring that I believe it has a commercial
value, and if you stop buying my book, I think

that to make a living I will bottle it and sell it
for a table water. You will know it by the following verse on the label, to help, not hinder,
the sale of a delightful draught from the hills : —

Whence come I?
Hastening down the mountain-side,
    Where the green ferns love to hide,
Underneath the sycamore shade,
    Through the cañon's grassy glade,
        Thence came I.

A MORNING DRIVE

"WELL, comrade, do you feel sufficiently rested after your long overland journey to take a twenty-mile drive this morning?"

"Yes, indeed, I am more than myself. This Ponce de Leon air renews my youth."

"Permit me, then, to give you a local synonym for happiness. It is this, — a pair of strong bay horses in a light Concord wagon that 'talks,' which you are driving over a long stretch of beach on the hard sands, at the lower-low tide, exploring some of the wooded cañons en route; then, passing over Point Duma, you will end the morning in Zumaland."

"I will allow the synonym, provided you put it to proof. Let us go."

Through the sycamores, over the green valley lands, on toward the beach we went, the horses entering into the spirit of the occasion. It is useless to say it was a day of days. That almost goes without saying in Southern California. The ground squirrels scampered off at our approach; the ground owls flew away in alarm, their great eyes flashing and glaring. He who has seen one of these burrowing owls drop a courtesy has seen a very laughable

thing; and whoever has noticed a boy rushing
forward to catch one, on the foolish supposition
that owls cannot see in the day, has beheld a
sadly disappointed lad when the owl took to
flight.

As the wheels crushed down the sand em-
bankment at the beach-side, and we found ourselves at Ocean's Edge, in admiration of the
scene we stopped our horses.   Yonder, across
the blue bay, a high mountain stood, proud with
its crown of snow; to the southward, Catalina
Island loomed up in splendor.   Behind us were
the green fields and the brown mountains,
while in either direction to our right or left
there lay a long stretch of beach.   This coast
offers inducements for the building of a road
well-nigh equal to Italy's famous Cornice Road.
If Ocean Avenue were extended from Santa
Monica to Hueneme, the days of coaching
would come back, for the attractions of such a
route would compel patronage.

But there are so many delightful drives hereabout, it is sometimes as difficult to select your
drive as to choose the prettiest color in a rainbow, or to hit a flying swallow, or to catch a
piece of paper in a whirlwind.

Driving over the hard sand by the side of
the sea is so exhilarating, inhaling the life-giving ozone as we go along!   Hear the cracking
and popping of the kelp pods as the wheels
break them!   Now the road leaves the beach

and takes up on to the mesa. Mesas are
elevated level lands; flat hills, if you will.
Rolling along over the mesa through the alfilaria, the air is redolent with the musk this
precious grass exhales when in bloom. Suddenly a road-runner, head down, darts out from
some bushes, and taking to the road ahead of
us the bird proves his name. How he can run!
They are great snake-killers.

The derivation of the name of this succulent
and valuable native grass will interest us.
"*Alfilar* is the Spanish word for pin, *alfilarilla* being the diminutive, that is, little pin.
Because of the resemblance of its seed spikes
to small wooden pins, the Spaniards dubbed it
alfilarilla. The ll being nearly silent, the American, spelling by ear, writes it *alfilaria*, and this
in turn has been shortened into *filaree*."

The lively horses speed on, descending again
to the beach, and after a bit of shore leave it, to
carry us up into Soston Cañon, where the road
winds among the sweet bays, the water oaks, and
the black alders, until the nestling hamlet is
seen by the side of the singing brook, where we
stop for a drink from a mineral spring. Back to
the beach still again, only to leave it after a mile
or so, to drive into the woodlands of Escondido
Cañon, at whose head we come face to face
with a great precipice of rock over which falls
the Escondido Cataract. *Escondido* means hidden, and this beautiful gem is indeed hidden

away. Without a guide you would never find it. On the face of the wall of the precipice two white sulphur springs exude their waters, coloring the rock, while all about the base of the pool are masses of maidenhair fern, growing even up the sides of the cliff. A sycamore tree bends over as in benediction. We leave this fern-side, silent, until by mutual impulse we begin singing "Hiding in Thee."

Coming down the cañon the horses sniff the sea, and again we startle the sea fowl having a congress on the sands. Bowling along we soon reach Duma anchorage, where the road leads up on to the rolling hills of Point Duma. The broad, cattle-dotted pastures are spread before us.

Modest little road birds, just the color of the highway, are here feeding; while sailing high above us, the buzzards, coarse and vulgar, are scenting carrion. But they deserve better adjectives; these useful birds devour all offensive dead flesh. They are nature's scavengers. In Charleston, South Carolina, I have seen them eating refuse that would otherwise taint the air. There it is against the law to kill them.

"Yes, friend, the gathering buzzards, circling high, proclaim the death of one of my herd. Rarely have I seen an animal protecting its own dead. Once I saw a steer driving off with his horns some buzzards that sought to light upon his dead comrade ox, prostrate by his side."

The Bible becomes another book to a transplanted resident of Southern California: so many biblical references are here reproduced. For instance, the prophet Jeremiah declared, by inspiration, that those who, at a particular time, turned from the living God and dwelt in wickedness, should not see burial, but that their bodies should be left to be devoured by vultures.

Up and down the hills the road leads us, until, passing the cactus circle, we come in view of the fair Zuma Valley below, — our destination. We now pass across a mustard hillside, delighted with such decoration of the landscape, and one of us says : —

> The hills so bright with mustard,
> Aye! that's a sight to see;
> The woad-waxen of New England
> Would not so well please thee.

What is that sound of warbling birds ? See, it is a flight of goldfinches. They alight on the mustard branches, and many little fellows fastening to a single branch bend it low.

We are now on the brink of the grade, and, setting our brakes hard down, we descend into the Zumaland among the sycamores.

This vale the cattle and birds and wild flowers have preëmpted. We cannot jump their claims, but perhaps they will not forbid our resting here awhile. Here the great-hearted meadow larks lift their voices high to heaven, almost bursting their yellow throats for joy.

Here sings the red-winged blackbird, whose warbling note is incomparable in its fullness; it is liquid music indeed. See his "epaulets." Here in Southern California we have white-wing blackbirds, too.

Your feet can tread the most beautiful wild-flower rugs. Salmon-colored this one is, in that little nook amid the bushes. Here are rugs of cream-cups, baby-blue-eyes, and of the gorgeous poppy, the prince of the foothills and the pride of the people. The sheen of the poppy petal is almost as wonderful as the brilliancy of its color. Its botanical name is Eschscholtzia. This was bestowed upon it by the botanist Chamisso, in honor of his friend Dr. Eschscholtz, who came to America in 1816 with an exploring expedition, as its surgeon.

Now we unhitch our team, stake out our horses on the wild grasses, and seat ourselves under a noble old sycamore for — meditation? Ah no, because a set of raucous-cawing crows disturb our peace. There seems to be a colony of them overhead. Yes, yes, noisy ones, we will leave; we should not have come here had we known that the memory of that last lark's song would be spoiled by your hoarse croaks. We will go over there, hear a respectable bird sing, and rest under another tree.

This lovely Zumaland lies close beside the sea. 'T is the fairest valley of all those that grace these wonderlands. High mesas rise on

either side guarding this nature's shrine.   Great
mountain crags form its background, while
around the vale groves of branching sycamores,
like sentinels, stand.

> The trees a circle make about thy graciousness,
> As halo round a holy countenance.

Seen in February sunlight who shall dare say
any other little valley can compare with this?
Who but God could have wrought its beauteous
site and curving hills?   Fair Zumaland! the
race of men whose tribal name was thine, cross-
conquered, is gone forever.

Farewell, Zumaland, farewell!   Thy pristine
beauty may soon vanish like the Zuma tribe.
Thy alfilaria will yield her ancient acres to the
barley, and thy sycamore will fall to the woodman's hungry axe.   Thy site alone shall live
to declare the greatness of thy virgin glory, as
God, unhindered by the hand of man, created
thee.   The mountains and the ocean defy man's
effort; they will stand.   Blest is the man who
has thus known thee, — as to-day.

Let not sadness seal thy smile, fair Zumaland.   'T is beautiful to exist for beauty, but
't is noble to live for usefulness.   So hail the
axe, and bless the plough, whose share shall
bruise thy brow, fair Zumaland.   Rejoice that
thou couldst serve the chosen creatures of thy
Creator, e'en at such a cost.

But no; on second thought, and through the
advice of a friend, it seems best to keep Zuma

as a park, and to tell the axe and plough to keep off the sycamore and alfilaria. So you can come, kind reader, and see it as it is, at your convenience. Zuma! to be in thy presence makes one happy; it makes one feel like singing, — nay, it makes one sing : —

> God grant that peace may ever be
> In Zumaland beside the sea.

With a lingering farewell, we leave Zumaland. The wheels, themselves reluctant to depart, again turn, and we are homeward bound. And it was well we left when we did; for majestic thunderheads were creeping up from behind the mountains, and before we got home we had a race with a rain cloud; the forewarning cloudlets had sent their shadows across the growing barley fields.

Soon the blue smoke rising from the home chimney was a welcome sight. It told of cheerful faces, glowing firesides, and good cheer within. Blessed is the man who has another to toil for his welfare and strive for his love, even as he toils and strives for her.

> So a God-speed to the husband, God-speed to the wife;
> May they live ever happy to the end of their life.

DESOLATION AND CHARITY

THE DRY YEAR

"Good-morning, neighbor; what think you of the weather? Have you noticed the malva curling up this early? That is a *good* sign for a *bad* year."

"Yes, comrade, it is a dry year this time, sure enough. No more rains of any account this year."

"Have you enough feed to carry your stock through?"

"No, I fear not. I shall sell my calves, steers, and old cows, and try to make it with the balance."

"How is your corn coming on?"

"Pretty small, I tell you; if I get a tenth of a crop I shall feel content."

Such conversations precede the bitter experiences of the long, dry months that follow a great lack of winter rains. There was a dry time in 1863, another in 1877, and in 1897 there was a great drought. In November, 1863, there was a regular downpour, and it did not rain again until November, 1864; and in consequence, dead cattle covered the ground from Monterey to Southern California. Abel Stearns' losses in cattle were enormous. The year 1877 was very dry. In Santa Barbara county, hay was forty dollars a ton. I have heard men say, with a sigh, " It was the dry year of '77 that broke me up. My sheep all died." Many a man grew gray that year, as he saw his living withering away.

Alas ! alas ! the dry year is upon us. The very air seems oppressed and oppressing. It is a battle to feel cheerful when Nature is sad. One's nervous system loses its elasticity, and it is hard to do vigorous work. Indeed, this may be the effect of the mind upon the body : the mind being burdened with distress, the body responds sympathetically. The sombre fields look sad and discouraged. The wild flowers are not " in tune," but lie late, sleeping silently in the seeds ; the poppy fields are silent and sad, though next year they will awake in their glory. The cows, with mournful pity, look upon their shrunken-sided calves ; the mothers eat even the leaves, but alas ! they make but little milk. The goats drop their young before time, in the foothills, for lack of nourishment to support their growth. Dejection is on every side. Even the good spirit of the blue jay seems lacking, under the relentless skies.

In this " day of grief and desperate sorrow," what shall we do but trust in God ? Our cattle and horses have death before them. The little lambs lie dead about the corral and on the hills,

the ewes being milkless. To pay the pasturage
on alfalfa farms would cost more than the stock
is worth. The mountain pastures are all occupied. Many have taken their cattle out on the
desert, which, by the way, in Southern California is not a Sahara, but abounding in nutritious
forage. To pay freight to distant ranges is im-
possible. Our barley seed, bought with our
own hard-earned wages, came up but to die.
We have no hay for our work horses; no income awaits us from the sale of butter, since
there is no herbage; and how shall we buy the
feed for our chickens? Ah, pity the farmer in
the dry year! Come to his help, butchers! Buy
those of his cattle that are eatable, at prices
prevailing before the market was overstocked
with cattle in view of the dry year. Aid him,
ye city dairymen! Keep his cows for their milk
till the windows of heaven are opened again,
and showers fall.

Men are discouraged. Those without living
faith cry, "Woe! woe!" And many are the
prayers that ascend to heaven — "O Lord, send
rain" — from lips which in good seasons forget
to praise Him for the showers. A dry year
makes men think of God. At such a time you
can know who are Christians indeed; for such
cry not, "Woe, woe," but, "His will be done."
They say God sends the dry years for some
wise purpose; perhaps because men have failed
to fulfill his ancient law, that every seventh

year they should rest their lands, and should
lay up store and forage for that sabbatic agri-
cultural year. One philosopher has said that
"every country suffers periodically from either
too much or too little rain. The land in this
State never gets a rest until a dry year gives it
one." If the ground had been rested, according
to God's command, this doubtless would not
have come to try the hearts of men. God will
not be mocked.

Yes, when the dry breath of the north wind
curls up the slight herbage, and hope would
seem to leave his heart, our hero stops, and
sings, "In some way or other the Lord will provide ; God will raise up some means to deliver
his children who have loved Him." So, when
the barley comes up and the fields put on a
tinge of green only to wither away into useless-
ness, still *his* hope abides.

Word came from Ventura to-day that a man
up the valley had shot all his range horses rather
than see them die, for he could not sell them.
Another rancher, with a flock of seven thousand sheep, has found it necessary to kill two
thousand young lambs, in order to save the
lives of the mother sheep. They are taking
horses to the soap-works, and selling them at
two dollars and a half. The hide is worth a
dollar and a half, the tail fifty cents, and the
balance is valuable for soap and land dress-
ing. Some cannot pay their interest, and the

mortgage is foreclosed.   Others, more prudent,
rejoice that they had kept to the motto their
parents taught them, "Out of debt, out of
danger."

In Little Bear Valley a band of fifteen hundred sheep has been abandoned by the owners,
because they had no feed.   In some places the
oak-trees were cut down to let the cattle
browse off the branches and moss.   Oh, the soil
is so dry.   In vain do we dig down for water.
There is no dew on the morning ground.   The
morning grass burns with fire, for there is no
moisture in the air to make dew.   When the
clouds come there is no rain in them.   Happy
and wise is the man who has settled by a
water-course, who owns a never failing spring,
or whose wind-mill is above real water-bearing
ground.   The streams never were so low.
They sink before they reach the sea.   The
very ocean bewails his ungratified thirst.
Truly, water, thou art king, with full power
of awakening the apparent dead.   In another
way art thou the emblem of truth ; for as Christ,
the King, possesses awakening power, so dost
thou over the waiting seeds.

Californian who hast known a dry year, fail
not to read Jeremiah xiv. 3–6, and for further
peace of mind and counsel do not forget to read
Jeremiah xiv. 22, Isaiah lviii. 11, and Habakkuk
iii. 17, 18.

Many laborers stand idle in the market-place,

for there is no harvest to handle.   The store-
keepers in vain exhibit their wares.   People
have no money with which to buy anything
save the real necessities. All honor to the city,
or the man of means, who will now make work
for the poor.

But, kind reader, even dry years come to an
end.

> " Some day the clouds will surely gather,
>   And you will want your green umbrella."

See, the clouds are getting heavy! the rain
has come.   The precious drops are diamonds
in value.   "God has not forgotten us," the
Christian cries ; and with sullen glee the unbe-
liever examines his gang-plough.

No one who has not lived through the long
summer and autumn California months can
understand how welcome the first rains are.
How eagerly the ranchmen scan the skies and
note the wind!   The air becomes charged with
vital electricity.   The storm breaks upon a willing people.   The trees bend to the breeze and
toss their happy heads.   One can almost see
the thirsty soil look up to the sky with smiles
of gratitude. .The dust flies in anger because
its reign has ended.   Its reign is dead !   Long
live the rain !

THE MOUNTAIN FIRE

In September comes the danger from mountain fires.   This applies not to the valley men,

but to the mountaineers, whose homes are high in the hills. The fierce northeast wind begins to blow. Now some cruel-hearted and selfish man, thinking only of his own gains and forgetting the injuries he is about to perpetrate on his neighbors, fires some dry brush that the wind-driven fire may clean some brushy mountain slopes, where next year his cattle may find a greater space for pasturage.

Crackle! crackle! burns the brush. "It is only going to burn over a few acres," Satan whispers to the criminal. Crackle! crackle! But now the terrific wind assumes control of the blaze, and, with a swift-sweeping rush, the fire speeds onward in its deadly course. The wind and the fire race as for life. The deer, the birds, the quail, and the rabbits, in an agony of fright, fly to escape death, too often in vain.

The fire has now leaped into his neighbor's lands. The cattle, seeing the flame from afar, as if by intuition run for the ocean beach or some safe place. The horses, unlike the cattle, stand trembling, as if awed by the danger, and sometimes are rooted to the spot until a horseman drives them away to safety.

But the flames do not stop. The death wind has three days to blow, and does not dream of ceasing. To the farmers and the mountaineers the vibrating air is sounding the death knell of their hopes. Fling open the gates that the cattle may escape from the coming fire! Set back-fires if it be not too late to protect the improvements! Hurry, be quick and put wet blankets and gunny sacks on the haystack side exposed to the flying firebrands. Mother! get the children together; put the Bible and our keepsakes in a sheet and start for the creek. It is your only hope. And the farmer, counting the sweat cost of those hundreds of post-holes he dug, is almost overcome with dismay, as he realizes his miles of fencing are soon to be burned, his home, his harvest, his earthly all is about to be consumed. But no time is there for further thought. With his family he flies to the clearing at the creek, and the fierce flames pass them by as if in anger at having lost their prey.

As soon as the heat will permit he goes back to his own once smiling farm. Now the fields and pastures are black in death. His house, his hay, his improvements and fencing are no more. The saddened family, too bereaved to cry, start down the mountain-side in search of food and shelter. And this man is but one of many.

Oh, for the power to write a Ramona book to arouse sentiment against our forest fires! What legislator will frame a prohibitory law against thus firing the brush? How great ought the prison penalty to be! These fires

affect our watercourses, and so the common-
wealth.

The unfortunate farmer descends the slopes
to the foothills.   On his way he sees the
mountain quail, the little birds, the mountain
rats and coons, the snakes and badgers, dead
on the ground.   They met their Pompeii in
that dreadful flame.   Further down he comes
upon a band of his horses, their hair singed,
and now the tears come with manly flow; his
spirit breaks as he beholds a herd of his cattle
bunched together on a blackened hilltop, their
eyes distressed.   Can anything appeal more
strongly to the sympathies?

THE ASSOCIATED CHARITY

The dry year and the mountain fire just
about ruined one of the settlers on a government claim.   But he had friends.   From far
and near they gathered together, acting upon
a suggestion of a mountain saint, and each was
requested to bring something for a woodland
feast in the great sycamore grove.   Besides
this, each one was asked to give a dollar towards a purse to be presented to the unfortunate family, to help them get a new start.
Moreover, it was pleasantly agreed that the
recipients should organize a like benefit for
the next man burned out; thus all feeling of
being an object of charity was removed.

The day was delightful; the grove was in

its glory of foliage, and a great company was there. Of course there was a barbecue. Some wagon boxes, taken off and turned upside down, and covered with bright green ferns for a table-cloth, served as the banquet - boards. The sweet odors from the fires, here and there, told of the rare viands and the home talent. What a museum that feast was! One had brought a fattened angora kid, another a quantity of quail and a solitary cottontail rabbit. Then there were clams and crawfish, pompano and fresh sardines, wild honey from the high bee-caves, a haunch of venison and a wild goose, salted native almonds, ripened olives, and such bread and butter to eat with the sparkling rainbow trout!

There was much good-natured pleasantry, the most memorable being the bringing of two live ducks in a gunny sack, and their conditional presentation to a young man who had been blind from his birth. He was to have the ducks if he could, by feeling, guess the contents of the sack. He was a bright lad, and when he felt the broad bills of the ducks, — "Ducks!" he exclaimed, and thus won the prize.

Oh, yes, it was a great day, and everybody was happy, except a few who could not make the course of true love run smooth, and the one man who once *tried* to be a lawyer, and who was always complaining and trying to make people miserable; indeed, he would have blamed Homer because he had not written in English.

But before harnessing up, resolutions were passed, without a dissenting voice, that it was a great success, and when the wagons were leaving the grove you could hear naught else but happy calls of "Come and see us," "Come and see us."

IN THE SADDLE

A RIDE IN THE HILLS

BICYCLES are well enough for Kansas and for city life, but for mountainous regions, for the ups and downs of out-of-door life in Southern California, the Mexican-broken saddle horse should ever be given the palm. When I compare the merits of my Columbia and my Geronimo, the intelligence and vivacity of the latter are arguments away over and above all that can be said in support of the former. It is true the bicycle does more muscular good; but, on the other hand, the horse keeps one out of the office much longer. As the battle seems to some so even, we will compromise and agree to take half our outings in the saddle, and half on the saddle. But as this chapter deals with life in the saddle I must get into it at once, — into the chapter, I mean.

"It's a fine day for a ride in the hills. What say you? Will you add pleasure to my work by accompanying me on my rounds, for I have to count the cattle to-day? And it is no small task to learn if any out of several hundred are missing. You will see a typical stretch of

California country to-day. Yes? Then come
with me. Take the bright bay and I will
ride the hardy roan. Let us be Arabs together."

Soon we were up high in the hills, following
an old Indian trail, now loping over the mesa,
now riding up the cañon bridle-paths, across
the barrancas, over to another point of vantage where we could spy the cattle. Entering
the number of each bunch in our stock book,
now and then dismounting to re-cinch and put
the saddles again in place on the horses' backs,
talking many talks about this and that, once
picking up some fine specimens of reddish sparkling crystals, admiring the views in countless
variety as we rode, we at last came to the highest point in our day's route. And here a great
and marvelous sight was to be seen. The fog
clouds had been drifting in from the sea, and
were now a solid mass below us, entirely ob-
scuring the ocean, whose surf, however, we
could distinctly hear through the fog, beating
on the beach. Above us was clear sunshine.
Below was the great fog bank; it looked like
a floor of snow, or a mighty sea of soft snow,
or great areas of fluffy cotton batting. Just
then, with startling suddenness, we heard a
steamer's fog whistle, the ship not far away,
yet undiscernible.

And soon, wind driven, the land breeze blew
the fog away and it went out to sea, its edge

looking like a great wall; and over yonder was the steamer!

On and on we rode, through picturesque cañons, under the oaks, until we emerged on fair Soston's peak. From this summit are matchless marine and mountain views. We said there was nothing human about that vista; it was divine.

"Ah, Italy, thou hast a rival!" said John Harvard, as we took a parting glance from the saddle at these scenes and out over the sweeping sea.

That day we saw three deer; and later several coyotes who were devouring a dead sheep. The shepherd's dog often drives the coyotes away from their prey; but once an encounter occurred at a distance from Jules, the herder; there was a sharp fight, and the valuable dog was badly bitten in the neck. If you should see him to-day you would find his collar covered with sharp steel spikes. Now, Mr. Coyote, come on! You shall not kill my twenty-dollar Peter, — not in this land of inventions.

As we rode we saw a coyote catch a squirrel, which could have escaped had it been more watchful. Our dogs chased the coyote, who, doubling on the dogs, escaped into his den. God has given every creature enemies, and also a way of escape. Mankind's enemies are numerous, Satan in myriad forms; but in Christ we can escape, — we can escape into the cleft of the Rock of Ages, just as the coyote found his deliverance in the cleft of the rock. But we must be more watchful than the poor squirrel of our narrative, or we, too, shall be lost.

Coyote is from the Aztec *coyotl*, which means "the burrower."

Now the trail leads downward over a mountain-side. It is a well worn cattle trail. As a rule, if you want to lay out a road up on to a high mesa follow the cattle trail. The cattle are fine civil engineers. We pass into the brush at the base of the hill; a cottontail disturbs the sage and is gone almost before he comes in sight. Look out! Halt! There's a rattlesnake! Hear him sing with his tail. He is getting ready to spring. Look out for your horse's legs!

"Is there any gold in these mountains?"

"No, I think not; the formation is not right for gold. It has been well prospected," I replied.

"Tell me the story of California gold."

"On the authority of a pioneer of 1841, Mr. I. L. Given, Don Abel Stearns had in that year a quart bottle full of gold dust, which was obtained at the San Fernando diggings. Other statements point to the fact that as early as 1833 gold was found in the Los Angeles and Santa Clara valleys. Still another statement is that the San Fernando placers were found by Francisco Lopez, in 1842; while he was

pulling the blue-blossoming wild onions he discovered the dust golden at their roots.   In
those early days quartz mining was also
modestly carried on in the San Fernando
mountains, the Mexicans using the primitive
arrastre for a crushing-mill.   As for the great
discovery of gold in 1848, which turned the
world's eyes upon our State, it happened in this
way.   James W. Marshall was in charge of the
building of a new grist mill.   Captain Sutter
was the man who furnished the money, and
Marshall supplied the experience.   In the water
at the mill-race Marshall had frequently noticed
shining specks in the sand and gravel, and on
the morning of January 19, 1848, he found a
good-sized nugget.   This find was followed by
others, and soon the world knew what God had
hid for us in our mountain ranges.   Since then
on the desert, as well as elsewhere, gold has
been discovered.

"I have Captain Sutter's machete," I continued ; "it is a finely engraved Toledo blade,
his name, Captain Sutter, being thereon.   His
medals, silver cup, sabre, and correspondence
from several of our civil war generals, when
they were yet captains, I have also.   What
a pity it is there is no fireproof museum building in Los Angeles, — there are so many treasures of the past that should be preserved, and
be teaching and interesting the people of the
present.   The Portland Vase of the Aztecs is

owned in Santa Monica; I think it the finest earthen jar ever found in our country. Many a family has some historical object which would help to make a museum possible.

"But before I leave the story of our gold, I should tell you two things that are of interest. The first gold ever taken East from California arrived in Boston on May 7, 1849, on the ship Sophia Walker, Captain Wiswell. She carried about $80,000 in gold. The second fact is this: it is said the largest nugget of gold ever discovered in the United States was one found at Carson Hill, Calaveras County, in 1851. It was worth $43,534."

Now, lest I lead astray some eager youth, let me close my gold remarks by stating that it has been said that more money has been spent for supplies, wages, and time in hunting for gold than ever was taken out of the treasure boxes of nature.

"But come, companion, let us dismount and eat of our bread and olives, while the horses rest and enjoy these mountain grasses."

"My appetite consents."

So we uncinch and remove the saddles and bridles. With our riatas we tether the horses out on the untouched burr clover and bunch grass. Soon they cool their sweating backs by rolling on the inviting herbage.

After luncheon we rest awhile for our siesta; a gentle calm steals o'er us; we are too happy to talk.   It is a sleepy, growing day.   As I lie stretched out on the grass my half-opened eye catches sight of a beetle climbing the dizzy heights of a spear of ripe grass, to gather the seeds at the top.   See! he loosens the seeds which drop to the ground.   Then he slides clumsily down the blade of grass, finds the seed, and flies home with it to his granary.

Blessed is the man who, alike in the serenity of such surroundings and amid the murmur of distresses, has such control over his mind that he can dismiss all crowding, warring thoughts, and, listening to the sounds of nature, be in complete harmony with them.   Happier he who can not only do this, but also cast all his care on Christ and thus commune with nature's God.

The horses' drowsy heads drooped in their contentment; it was too bad to arouse them again for work.   But soon we were in the saddle and away.   The motion was made, seconded, and carried that before continuing the count we should go up the cañon and make a cabin call on the old mountaineer, who lived hard by, the bells of whose cows we could now hear, each answering unto each.

THE OLD MOUNTAINEER

He welcomed us to his hearth-stone, a great flat stone of prodigious size, and his especial pride.   When I said, " That makes a fine hearth," — "Aye, indeed, it does," he answered, satisfaction shining in his face. He was a bachelor, and had just finished his dish-washing; he had offered us home-made chairs, bottomed with skins of the snarling badger; wild-cat rugs were round about; the chief carpeting before the bed was the skin of a fine mountain lion he had shot the year before, when his faithful dog had treed it. His cat Tom was a treasure; he would often catch a rabbit, and when seen with such fine prey his master would say, "Here, Tom, you can't have all that; share and share alike." Thereupon Tom would give up the rabbit, and in due time receive his portion.

Within the cabin was the usual mountaineer's bricabrac, — antlers, a dried road-runner's skin, a quail's egg, and the tanned hide of a rattlesnake, with rattles, on a shelf in the corner. He said he always kept the fat of the rattlesnake, as it was "way up" for his rheumatism. Then on a little table was an ancient stone mortar full of agates, fossils, shells, and flint arrow-points. All these treasures were as dear to his heart as are the Sèvres vase and the Hawthorne bowl to the aristocrat.

In reply to an interrogation, he told us those dried-looking things hanging up by the fireplace were the galls of polecats, which he sold to the Chinese physicians for half a dollar apiece. His nose nerves were strong enough to enable him to pursue this calling.

He was kindly communicative, and was enthusiastic over his spring, whose waters were soft enough, he said, to properly cook beans; much Southern California water is not fit to cook beans mellow. All sorts of wisdom passed his lips. Now he was saying, "Everything that grows down plant in the dark of the moon, everything that grows up plant in the light of the moon;" and then again, "Boys, when you hunt in the last quarter of the moon remember the deer feed late into the morning. Then's the show to get a shot."

He told us his shoes cost him ten dollars a year, his clothes ten, and his living expenses were five dollars a month. "I can live finely on two hundred a year. Boots are the worst, I have to wear out so many. I eat fifty pounds of beans a year, but I raise those." His swine thrived on the wild oak acorns and the indigenous roots thereabout.

To dwell on a high mountain gives one a certain sense of elation that is invigorating. This you could feel in his presence. I have seen his face beam with true trapper's anticipation as he went out to tend his fox traps. He was lithe and strong; he could climb a mountain as easily as does a shadow. He knew all the various mountain bird voices. Where the quail hid, and where the rarest wild flowers loved to grow, he knew. He was familiar with all the by-trails through the dense chaparral. He knew what made the sheep and goats die so suddenly on the range, — that it was the poison of the milkweed; and quickly would he cut down all he saw on the range before the flocks came to graze. The habits of the deer were as a boy's alphabet to him. The constellations were his friends; he watched for their evening advent, and by the starry heavens was his little-tutored mind increased in faith. Ah! he was a rare comrade; his was a friendship worth having.

When he heard the voices of the night, the calling of the flying wild geese, he thought, Ah, a storm is in progress in a distant land. In the morning he would say, "The storm will come; the geese said so. Besides, the smoke goes not far above the chimney top."

He remembered how Andrew Sublett in 1854 had his arm broken by a grizzly bear in the Malibu Cañon.

He brought to mind how his old colored neighbor across the range had been maltreated by the settlers, on account of his color; how they set fire to his cabin, hoping thus to terrorize him and to drive him from the country; how some thought the real purpose was that some men with white faces and black hearts wanted to jump his claim after they had got rid of him. But this was not the material the good old gentleman was constructed of, and, as a shame to his tormentors, he put up a sign over the ruins of his cabin which read: "This was the work of the Devil."

Once he helped me kill a lynx that I had run down on horseback, and had driven under an old sycamore log. Having no gun I did not know what to do, but my good friend, happening along, found a club, and, telling me to stand on one side, he struck him again and again, as the sharp-eyed lynx scowled and growled underneath the inclined log. At last the fatal blow fell, and I have his hide, salt-and-ashes tanned, for a rug.

That day the conversation turned to rattlesnakes, and the old mountaineer told us this winter-fearing reptile's trail was always curved, while a gopher snake makes a straight track. He knew the rattlesnake weed, of which the Mexicans make a pulp to bind on to snake-bite wounds. He told us how the road-runner offers battle to the rattler; how "with caution he approaches his enemy, stretching one wing down as a shield and waits for the snake to strike. The wing is thrown to catch the bite, and, as quick as a flash and before the snake can recover, the runner with unerring aim sends his long beak, hard as ivory, through the head of his antagonist." This language is not mine, but Captain Lapeyre's.

For eight months and over the rattlesnake will live without food. How good of God to have made this venomous serpent of a different color from the grass! The non-poisonous gopher snake is, on the other hand, not easily seen, owing to his color. Providence!

"Come up to the fern pool," our host said; and we walked there, two hundred yards from his house. Here was a sweet spring basin in a nest of ferns, with fresh green shrubs. Its beauty was marred by a water dog gliding across its waters. This water lizard seems out of place in beautiful Southern California, but of course he is not; in some way he has a mission. All loveliness has a lack in it somewhere. The repulsive water dog proves the rule that perfection is not found in earth's nature kingdom. It awaits us above.

The long pipe-stem lizards sunned themselves near by, but they are not very harmful; they are so called because, if struck by a stick, their tails fly into as many pieces as a pipe stem when broken on the pavement. The common little lizards are harmless, sometimes being even used for pets. I do not like to recall the remembrance of a lady in Saint Augustine, Florida, I once knew, who had such a creature for a pet, feeding it regularly and taking it in her hand. A Californian I have known who would catch them, put them on his shoulder, and let them run at will over his back. These things are told to ward off fears of poison. The big pipe-stem fellows, however, I will not vouch for.

COMING HOME

Bidding adios to our good friend, we continued counting the cattle. Riding over the sweet-smelling tar-weed flats is a delight peculiarly Californian. The air was scented with the perfume of wild flowers. We passed a field of wild coreopsis, so brilliant as to dazzle the eyes. We gathered a bouquet of mountain flowers, wild peonies, Pacific buttercups, and native forget-me-nots, with a bunch of shooting-stars. May the poet soon be born whose voice will be sweet enough to sing of the wild flowers of Southern California!

Some of these descriptions will seem strange to the winter visitor of Los Angeles. He will say, "I stayed in Pasadena a whole winter and I never saw a pelican nor picked a chocolate lily." Indeed? Neither did I ever see a business block in the woods. Tarry longer, stranger; come into the country, and know the land you live in.

Through tall reeds, eight feet high, their long feathery heads waving in the light wind, the trail took us. Gay blue birds were flitting about, their color so blue that it seemed as if they had dipped in the sea on a day when it borrows its hue from the deep blue of the sky. But now we are nearing home.

We ride down the green slopes of a landscape poetic; our task is done; the count is made.

As if to make a gracious finale to our happy day, a chorus of meadow-larks and merry linnets burst out in a concerto, as we come to the home-mesa.

If thou dost love music, come with me some time to a high mesa on a sunny morning, and inhale with the birds the freshness of the recent rain-wet ground. I will have a choir of a score of golden-breasted larks sing for you, just as they daily sing to the delight of the hills. Presently you will hear a solo of a single lark's trill. What do you think of that? Even the wind stopped to listen, it was so beautiful. See him as he turns in his flight and shows his gorgeous yellow breast, a burst of color.

When we took singing lessons we were told to open well our mouths. I think the author of that advice must have seen a skylark singing, for the lark opens his bill so wide that, at times, we fear it will be dislocated. Bird ability in music is wonderful. The deep liquid notes of the blackbird's sunset song: ah! those lower throat tones of a bird's voice no instrument can approach. What organ has a bird's warble-note stop?

We were going through the gate when my congenial companion said, " It has just occurred to me to wonder where the old mountaineer gets his annual ten dollars to pay for his boots."

"Bees," I replied. "He sells honey. His hives were behind the hill in a clearing."

TWENTY-FOUR SOUTHERN CALI-
FORNIA HOURS

THE moonlit night has gone. Now comes
the mystic early dawn, when the moonlight
merges into sunlight, and the sun subdues the
moon, which, though conquered, slowly retreats.
The full moon is sinking away in the west, for
it cannot bear the brightness of the glorious orb
of day. The planets come to the aid of the
moon, but the sun, rejoicing as a giant to run
his course, puts them all to flight. Aurora's
torch is kindled, and dawn is here!

'T is almost sunrise. Bright rays, heralds of
the day, have, with the speed of light, announced
the coming of the sun. The day-dawn, rival of
twilight in the estimation of poets, shows its
glimmering myriad tones of color in the eastern
sky. The fair dawn gradually grows into day;
the gradations are marked with changing colors.
A glow like a rainbow suffuses the earth's
surface as it turns toward the sun; then the
rose-colored sky is changed to a liquid yellow.
Soon the atmosphere becomes silvery and then
pearl white, until finally the sun, shining above
the horizon, ushers in the clear white daylight.
Over the mountains and over the sea the pene-

trating rays of light quickly travel, hunting out
the darkness and chasing it from every rincon
and cañon.   At this time the dawn lights,
which had put poetry into the hills and made
the marine scenes at their best, have vanished.
The artist or the poet has but a few moments
to catch impressions.   The violet hues, the
mountain purple and sea-green tints of a few
moments ago defy portraiture and make the
artist ardent, yet fearful of his inability to
reproduce.

The solemn stillness of the night is now
broken by the birds' daybreak chorus.   Such
a fine burst of welcoming applause in honor
of the approaching Sun!   The orioles sing the
loudest, and all the birds combine to make a
jubilee that once heard is not forgotten.   Now
comes fair morning.   The morning-glories on
the trellis seek to second, in their silent way,
the birds' welcome of the sun.   It is their
morning worship.   The sun must have a happy
life, since at every moment he is greeted in his
course by the songs of millions of birds, as his
rays first appear on that portion of the earth's
surface on which they sing.

The mist rises from the grasses which glis-
ten in the morning dew.   The blue kindling-
smoke also arises from yonder cabin, offering
incense to the acting source of life, God's dep-
uty.   The sun is the poor man's alarm-clock.
About his door the larks now rehearse their

arias. But the sun has work to do, — from romance he quickly hastens to realities, as life duties succeed marriage bells. A little while ago he was painting the hills and writing poetry on the sea; now he is putting springing life into waiting seeds, and making the herbage grow up higher into his smiles of warmth.

From now till eventide, except at the noon hour, "fierce labor all subdues;" man and nature have their sleeves rolled up and their overalls on. But the noontime is so restful here; after a good dinner the toiler rests himself on the ground, absorbing nature's narcotic. Half asleep, he hardly hears the goat-bells tinkling on the distant hills, nor does he note how the raucous note of a passing crow puts a false tone into the harmony of the hour. But habit is the toiler's master, and at one he awakes.

In the afternoon the quail coveys cautiously come out from their hiding in the brush shelters, and go forth to promenade and forage. Hear them chatter away as they lead out into the world their inexperienced brood. See their quick footsteps as they speed from bush to bush with "sudden sally."

This afternoon we are up on the mesa overlooking the valley and ocean, in the companionship of the mountains, waiting for the sun to set; watching for the picture the Creator will paint on the western sky. The setting sun begins to shoot his slanting rays. The sunset shades of color on the lower-low beach are Nature's work of art, her water-color. To-day the ruddy glow shames even Turner. Now the sun throws its radiant glory across the surface of the sea as a last caress, and is gone to brighten other lives. The sunsets, — oh, the sunsets of the Southern California coast wonderland! What beautiful lights and colors the sun bequeaths to twilight!

The evening star beams down its blessing. 'T is the sweet twilight hour. Gradually come forth the stars, now triumphant over the sun. Have you ever seen a star peeping over the ridge of a mountain, whose gaze seemed almost intelligent, as if it looked you through and through? The quiet deer has come forth from the chaparral, and, scanning in precaution his feeding-places, eats towards the hidden spring. The early evening mountain wind sings its gentle song to Twilight, and we rejoice that we live in a land where by day we breathe ocean's invigorating ozone, and by night the vivifying mountain air, rarefied and refreshing. The Maker of the life-giving wind is now returning to the fields of the ocean the breezes which have been blowing landward from the sea all the day.

From his hollow tree the hoot-owl flies, and woe be unto the careless field-mouse to-night. The mountain quail's call sounds distinct in the stillness of twilight. It is a pretty sight to see

the new broods of mourning doves under pa-
rental guidance, swiftly flying to the water-
courses for their evening draught, their wings
making melody to the listener's ear. It is
strange that such lovely birds should be en-
dowed with such sad voices; it is quite true
that God distributes his gifts equally. He is
no respecter of birds. The little birds now
sing their vesper hymn. And the hoot-owl
says, Amen! Amen! in his bass voice. If an
owl could sing, how well he could render,
"Rocked in the Cradle of the Deep." I wonder if David discerned in the songs of birds at
day-dawn and eventide praises to Heaven, and
so said for himself, "Morning and evening will
I praise Thee." These evening bird warblings
invite gratitude and repose.

On the rocks off the shore the shags stand
in rows, roosting, and up the creek the husky
crane goes cromping, seeking his night perch;
as he flies he passes the swift-winged night
hawk, who darts by him uncomfortably close.
The hawk with piercing cry salutes the approaching night. In search of birds smaller
than himself, he, coward, sails o'er the country, now skimming along the hillsides, now
mounting to the ridges after prey. As he
flies along, the terrorized day birds, perching
in the bushes for their night's rest, discern as
if by instinct his coming. They begin to utter
cries of alarm, and the silent hillsides awake

with inhabitants hitherto unheard. The little
birds were too watchful for their enemy, and
the night hawk speeds away for less careful
birds ; as he becomes lost to sight the alarm
ends, and the hillside resumes its stillness.

Now the cricket orchestra plays, while an
occasional strident locust adds to the confusion
of tongues made by frogs. Amid the chirping
of the crickets and the croakings of the frogs
the great owl tries to imitate the cannon's
sound in the anvil chorus. A loud-voiced
cricket seems to lead all the rest and set the
tune, which proclaims the death of day.

At twilight a restful calm settles down on
everything, as if nature was preparing to lose
itself in slumberland. All day-nature seems
to pause and rest, except the flowers, which
now best exhale their fragrance. The after-
glow of twilight is most beautiful; sometimes
a fair pink cloud is resting gently on the northern sky, a scene seraphic ; sometimes at this
hour the fog comes in from the sea like a
coverlet, with which to enfold the hills for the
night ; sometimes the crescent moon makes
serenity more serene.

Twilight is the hour when earth seems
nearest heaven. The summer twilight seems
to hold one spell-bound, and it is then one can
almost *feel* that God fills all space about one.
Children's minds are made receptive to the
truth by the peaceful air and the solemn quiet

at the close of day when toil ends and rest
begins.   These moments seem suited to relate
the prophetic teachings concerning the second
coming of Christ.   At eventide, children readily absorb the truths of salvation, and those
instructions which belong to the soul.   Hast
thou ever heard thy firstborn, on such a twilight, bear witness that he had been born
again?   "Bring up a child in the way he
should go, and when he is old he will not
depart therefrom."

In Southern California the summer twilight
is especially delightful, even more so than in
New England, because in the East, oftentimes,
the great heat of the day extends into the
evening; while by the Ocean of Peace, the
twilight is just cool enough.   Then the children, relieved of the strain of the day, find
themselves lively again, and happily flit about.
Watching for the evening star, he who dis-
covers it claims it for his own.   The mother,
erstwhile, sits contentedly by, playing sweet-
voicéd hymns on the autoharp, which was made
for twilight ; and the father notes down all
this on a scrap of paper.

> And now has passed the twilight,
> Friend of both day and night;
> The evening star will fade away,
> Abashed at the moon's full light.

The full round moon rises grandly over the
mountain, and glorifies the valley.   It broods

over the scene like a benediction; it makes you
think of the overshadowing of the Holy Ghost.

As the evening deepens, the silver moon becomes golden;
  Now night wraps her robe about her charge.

Sweet nature! Blessed night! without thee we
should perish; should the sun control thy
sphere as well as day, no flowers would there
be for us, no grain for our bread, nor herbage
for our kine, — all would be parched.   Ay,
God made the dark.   It is well to teach children the value of darkness, how their very life
depends on it; and then China must have sunshine as well as we; we should not be selfish.

But think ye the night has no dwellers? No
activities? No tragedies? Ah! while most of
nature sleeps, a part is awake. Night is day for
many! Gather your cloak around you, the bats
are about. Living in the country soon removes
dread of bats; "familiarity breeds contempt;"
it is the same with horses' hoofs and cows'
horns. The bats alone of the mammals have
wings. They are great destroyers of our big
mole crickets. Badgers and wild cats go out
into the night on their depredations, though
they cringe with fear at the sight of a puma's
track. Ah! you have no idea about what is
going on every night while you are asleep.

Nature lives on nature, and created things
eat creatures. No sooner have the rays of the
retreating sun sought other lands to bless, than
out from countless holes in rock and earth, cliff

and tree, thousands of eyes are peeping. Sir Coyote and Fox of fable fame now claim the land as theirs, and go forth destroyers. Owl and bat seek various vermin that hide their hideousness in night. Another set of owners own our wonderland, and happy are we if certain prized buff cochins are not devoured before the morn.

How I would like to borrow an owl's eyes for just one night! What vantage views of the nocturnal battle for bread I should then see! What revelations would be given of how even owls carry away poultry, and how the rabbits spoil so much of what honest hours have planted! At night you would see the polecat running along the kelp-line on the beach, searching for dead sea fowl and fishes cast ashore by the tide, holding high his pluméd tail when surprised. Hark, — the raccoon's distant call! The coyote bays the moon on yonder ridge.

Have you ever seen a cotton-wool, mackerel sky on a moonlight night? Is it not wonderfully beautiful? Do you remember how your new-mowed hay field absorbed a silvery sheen from the moon's rays? The moonrise over the mountains is a majestic sight. How many phases of beauty the moon has! The crescent with its attendant star is loveliness; at the moon's first coming it just peeps at our part of the world, bashful, showing only the outlines of its mighty grandeur in the dim distance. The second quarter of the moon is a period of even greater serenity in the midnight landscape scene than in the full glow of its whole light. But as for majesty, what save the sun can approach the awful power of the silver sovereign of the tides, the great search light of the heavens and earth. The mighty moon! Her majesty, the moon!

How fair are the fields of starland! The shining constellations, stationed by immutable law, their vigil keep, and guard the sleeping sons of men. Did you ever watch the heavens steadfastly at one point? At first you see only certain stars; a moment more you see other stars, before unseen, which are farther away; we can thus easily believe there may be still other stars in space thereabout, yet more distant, but which are invisible. Thus we can increase our faith in the fact of the existence of the heavenly land, — heaven. It is far above us, and so far as to be unseen save by the spiritual eye, which is only a function of the soul. What credit would there be if we could actually behold heaven and hell? We should be good through constant fear. God wants us to fear the consequences of his displeasure, but wishes us also to serve Him through love. If our physical eyes could see beyond the stars we should all get to heaven, but like the fallen, disobedient angel Lucifer, there would be many who would not have sufficient real love of righteousness ; and they would be thrust into hell for disobeying the laws of the golden streets, were it possible to disobey them.

We say the moon is so many million miles from our earth. By imagining the circumference of a circle, far greater than that of which the distance from the earth to the moon is the radius, we can easily grasp the idea that the greatness of heaven is certainly vast enough to provide eternal dwelling-space for millions of the redeemed, and for all yet so to be. It may be also for the redeemed of other planets beside our own. This drawing will explain these words.

The Lord bade mankind pray, " Our Father who art in Heaven." Men were so to pray in Boston and Canton, in London and Los Angeles. At every point men were to look upward, it seems, and feel that heaven was above their heads. Would not heaven thus be always above all men?

To increase thy faith, go out into a summer night, and, reclining, look upward to the dome of the heavens. Meditate upon the passage of thy redeemed soul, if it so be thou hast been born again, when, at the death of thy body, thy spirit flies through space, leaving behind all corruptible things, past the planets, onward, nearing heaven, till its mansion is safely reached. Ah, 't is a clear summer's night, that will lead the willing mind heavenward.

So have passed away the most of our twenty-four Southern California hours. Now come the still small hours of the night-time. There is a time when all is quiet, and the night voices cease. Even night sleeps. The crickets are silent, and the frogs are hushed. Silence reigns. A slight seismic tremor is felt; it shows while most of nature slumbers, God keeps a part awake.

The watch says it is time to close our chapter. I hope to-morrow will be a pleasant day.

THE MOUNTAIN CLIMB

"Over the hills the sun is climbing; soon on us it will be shining. Comrade, let us be boys again, and taking the hint from the sun, suppose we climb yonder high summit, stopping at the Pool of Silence on the way. You know from that peak you can look over into the valleys on the other side of the range and actually see the old Santa Barbara stage road."

"Agreed; I am for the climb."

As we mounted to the first foot-hills, we began to get a glimpse of the grander view awaiting us from the summit. Even here a lovely landscape greeted our delighted eyes. The air was commencing to be rarefied. In the hills one has such confidence in the atmosphere — its purity is unquestioned. We had passed the herds of grazing sheep; we had watched the Mexican boy, who, like David, by his sling directed the devious ways of the flock through the hills; casting a stone to the right of them if he wished them to go to the left, and *vice versa*. How restful it all looks! It is an old saying, that "where sheep are, there rest is."

It is remarkable how hungry for company

and conversation a sheep-herder will get, who stays with his flock alone and rarely sees people. I have often noticed, when I went up into the mountains, how he would approach me, and talk as eagerly as a hungry man devours food. I would let him talk away until he was talked out. I felt I had been of service to him.

We had heard the woodman's axe far on the mountain-side. We had rested at the base of an abrupt rise in the trail, stretching ourselves out on the strengthening ground. A certain strength and power or force can be absorbed from the ground. Go to a sunny hillside, and on the roadway cut around it, whose upper bank shall be a slant of at least four feet, *there* sit you down, your back against the bank. Let your whole length come in contact with the earth, including the palms of your hands. If you are weary from work, especially of a sedentary kind, it is astonishing how quickly your vigor is restored. Thus one can get balm and strength from the soil and promote longevity.

In these first foot-hills we discovered a paradise for the botanist. It was the only place in which I had found the yellow mariposa lilies, and red, purple and white ones too, of the same species. I know a bank whereon grows the rare chocolate lily, bell-shaped. Sometime I will show it to you, and you can get some seeds. Here were wild gardens of blue lark-

spur, which the Mexican calls the spurs of
Saint Joseph. Many white star-shaped lilies
bedecked the hills, just as if God in his love
had sprinkled the earth with answering stars,
to remind us of the starry heavens at night,
that the thought of man in the daytime, too,
might be gently led to Him.

"But come, comrade, we must imitate the
sun and keep climbing." This we did amidst
a change of flowers and shrubs. The button-
sage and the yerba buena now gave forth their
odors with aromatic pungency when crushed in
the hands. The wild pea and morning-glory
ran over the ground, and the bright red moun-
tain.pinks jeweled our paths. Level with our
faces were the blossoms of the mountain lilac,
the fairest of all. We were now getting into
the chaparral.

The trail now led downward, and passing
through thick brush descended to a little cañon,
whence it again ascended over great boulders
and a jungle of rocks, until we came to a most
beautiful spot, — a mountain spring, o'ershaded
by a spreading live-oak, in a natural reservoir
in the rock. Its outlet was a little stream
trickling down over a miniature precipice, at
the base of which you could stand and look
into the pool, almost even with your eyes.
Ferns grew about its sides, and birds and bees
sang its praises. When we first found it, we
said, What shall we call it? Long-life, Hygeia,

Seek-no-further, came into our minds, but we finally were satisfied with no name save the Pool of Silence; and so it is called to this day, as the historian would say. It is silent in the midst of the stillness and silence of the high hills. One can almost *feel* the silence there.

But the water itself ! Civilization is all right. It is very convenient, when it rains, to congratulate ourselves as we hold a glass under the faucet and drink therefrom the piped water ; but methinks a drink from a shady spring untouched by man, whose waters are tinged with the flavor of the fallen oak leaf, and the roots of the ferns growing by its side, together with a dozen other constituents, combine to produce a taste which is *sui generis*, and which is lost when the spring is cemented and roofed, and kindly nature shut out. Ah ! such pristine water is the nectar of the mountains, the wild waters of the hills !

We drank a last draught, and took to the trail, stooping to examine a puma's startling track. The way leads upward again, through the chaparral. From its dark green a bright blue jay comes into rare relief. How often have I hidden in the chaparral to rest, no eye to see me save that of God. The dark green mountain chaparral jungles are a never-to-be-forgotten feature of California mountain life. The Raymond excursionist does not find them in his itinerary.

Leaving these shadowy places, the trail emerges on to a rocky slope. Now the sempre-vivas adorn the rocky sides of the mount; the Spanish bayonets present arms as we pass along, their sharp spines jealously guarding their precious blossoms. The sempre-viva leaves are full of water, and on many a long mountain tramp has the wayfarer bitten and sucked them for moisture, when water was otherwise unattainable. Here grows the little caravalla plant, the dried leaves of which the mountain Mexicans use as a substitute for tea. Above us, high in air, sails a mighty condor, rarely seen in this country. On yon sharp rock the white-headed eagle watches from his lofty perch. About here, we leave the trail to get a luncheon of wild honey from the cliffs near by, out of the bee caves; and wonder whether John the Baptist so secured his food in Palestine.

Now the trail is hard to discern; it seems to come to an end in a little cañon cul-de-sac; but wait, — ah, here it is again, all right. See, it makes off at an angle up that slope; just as in life our way seems to be hemmed in with difficulties, when lo, God opens up another path, and away we go rejoicing, and ashamed that we doubted at all. Faith is no faith that believes only after seeing. Up leads the trail, steeper and steeper; and here we are at the summit. And what a surprise! Why, here is a high tableland, a mountain-mesa. Oh, what a scene is spread before us! Every feature of nature is here represented, I believe, except a volcano. A river, winding in the distance, is one of the most attractive features of a landscape, and here it is.

I began to say "What a lot of feed there is here for my goats —" when my friend stopped me short with the words, "Do not spoil the poetry of the scene by such a prose remark as that." How few people know how to combine poetry and common sense in their lives! And yet I like him ever so much.

Here we are, where the great hills lift high their heads. Over there are the Sierra Madre or Mother Mountains. Was not that a happy thought, to name the main range as being the mother of the lower mountains? A fine old Spanish idea! By the way, the highest mountain in Southern California is Grayback, in the San Bernardino Range, eleven thousand seven hundred and twenty-five feet in altitude.

The mesa on the summit table-land is a beautiful place; wild flowers like these heights. I have seen a great space all red, white, and blue; red with blossoms of Indian tassels, white with mariposa lilies, and blue with lupin. Truly, a patriotic garden. But to my mind a Southern California sight quite as beautiful is a mountain-side glorified with the wild lilac in full blue bloom. Would you expect to find a spring up so high? Yet there is one near by. We were athirst, so we began a search for water, which some willow-tree tops in a little cañada, hard by, promised. A willow tree is a signboard. The spring itself was approachable only through a maze of brush. It was guarded against discovery by resisting reeds, tripping blackberry vines, fierce nettles, poison oak, and a jungle of underbrush; with here and there a relentless buckthorn, whose young green bark we noticed had just been gnawed by a deer. In the midst of one great bush was a curious mountain-rat's nest, a mass of sticks and twigs, a maze of wonder. The undergrowth was so thick, and the thorns so sharp, that it all tended to discourage the discoverer, but a draught of such water rewarded the patient mountaineers.

Refreshed, we went back to the highest height and sat down, resting. "Does it seem," I said to my comrade, "that these great bulwarks of strength, these mountains, could ever be shaken in earthquakes? Sometimes we feel seismic tremors at our home way down below, in the valley. And yet I suppose these great mountains bend to the will of God, just as willingly as the little valleys. It is a lesson in humility. From these heights what a place to meditate on eschatology! What a vision from here would be the coming of the Lord! What a point of view from which to see the tumults of the last days, if it be that any one will have holiness enough to lift up his eyes.   Above the storm-rent clouds on high will the seven angels pour out the seven vials of the wrath of God, which may descend in thunderbolts of wreckage of things mundane.   Is it not written that, after great disturbances of nature and humanity, to crown all this majesty of divine wrath the Son of God shall appear in the clouds above us, as a Saviour from it all?   Has not Saint Luke written, 'when these things come, hold up your heads'?   Happy the man whose faith and conscience will be clear enough to hold up his head at that time.   Oh! comrade, what a celestial sight that will be ; what scenes in the skies there will then be, — Christ appearing with angels in the glory of the Father!   Who can grasp the fullness of the meaning of the glory of God?   The aurora borealis, the most marvelous marine sunset, the most wonderful sunrise scene among the snow-peaks of Switzerland, the most massive cloud-effects, — all fail to even approach what the glory of the Father must be.   And then canst thou not hear, in thy thought, the great trumpet of Heaven, and canst thou not so see our Lord deliver his judgments by the separation of the just from the wicked?

"Comrade, those three high peaks over yonder are named Conviction, Conversion, and Salvation Summits."

CONCERNING OUR SEASONS

"I DO not like Southern California, because the seasons are not distinctly marked," said an Eastern misanthrope one day. "There is too much sameness in your climate," the same party continued. "True," I replied; "we have no frozen water pipes, no March slush, no interruptions from elementary causes to travel, to telegraphing, or to commerce, save a few washouts of a day; we have no Oklahoma cyclones, our barns are not commonly struck by lightning, our citizens are not prostrated by sunstroke in August, our hats are not smashed in by falling ice from high buildings in winter thaws; but all the same we have a very reasonable climate. And as to 'sameness,' which you allege, why, our seasons have great variety. At the risk of telling you what you now know, let me remind you of a few of the changing conditions which concern our land as the months go by."

In Southern California we have decided seasons. Instead of white we have green; and while you Bostonians are rejoicing in green fields, ours are brown. Delightful as is the Southern California coast summer, yet still

more so is the winter; for then the green has
not gone to sleep, but freshness abounds on
every side.   The Eastern winter is the rest season for the earth; in California the summer is
when the unirrigated soil refrains from toil.
Now, is not green and brown, with geniality
in the air, superior to or at least the equal of
green and white with the mercury below zero?
Come, my pen, extol our climate!   Or at least
help me to recite some features of our passing
seasons, some that have impressed themselves
on my mind.

Behold, now, the yearly California miracle.
The first rains have come, — and gone.   The
whole country is suddenly changed from brown
to green.   Hope springs up with the seeds.   The
brown unsightly earth was strewn with unseen
seeds.   A copious rainfall comes, and lo! the
ground is wondrously green again.   The thirsty
soil opens its longing throat and great draughts
of water pour down into its vitals.   Cheered is
the ranchman's heart.   Well may he laugh.
Confidence grows apace with the wild grasses.
The thought of the harvest makes the task of
ploughing ahead of him seem light.   So does
the thought of bringing in our sheaves to the
Father make the toils and trials of life light.
Yes, what a relief to the farmer's heart are the
first rains.   How his smile comes back, how
his blood circulates with renewed vigor; what

a strain is removed from his mind. Now life seems well worth living, yes, there is no doubt about it !

The stock run about the fields with glee, although the large horses look askance at the gang plough. Cleansed is the ground, the sea refreshed, and the air purified. The skies, too, are relieved of their heavy burden, — the water-weighted clouds which hovered about for days before the rain. Faith in the future is the motto seen on every side.

Do you remember, in January, when the chaparral is in bloom on the foot-hills, how silvery and gray and green it looks in the slanting sunlight ? all those shades are com-mingled.

It is in the same month that the voice of the ploughman, urging on his horses in a neighbor-ing field, is borne by a favoring breeze to his neighbor's ears, and encourages him in his own task ; for noon is near and the team lags. He and they are thinking about their dinner. The ploughman notices and knows the various wild grasses that are just springing up ; he recog-nizes the individuality of each little leaf, he knows what it will be. "Welcome, red-tops ! Glad to see you again, 'filaree ! " The yielding sod of springtime is a pleasant cushion to the feet.

What an annual event it is when in March the orioles appear from some far country, with their talkative voices and bright colors.   Soon they begin to collect palm fibre for their ingenious nests.   Now the kill-deer plover in the arroyo fill the air with their cries of fright lest we should find their homes.

Now are the salutations of the lark most splendid.   Now comes the happy event when one of the family asserts to have seen the first blue-bird of the year.   Now the quail abandon their community custom, and go off two by two to set about their house-building.   Now begin to fly back to their early summer homes, to Goose Lake, and the farther northern feeding fields away beyond, great numbers of shag and sea-fowl.   If they could only talk, how much we could learn from their Arctic experiences!   If some one could only discover the Rosetta stone of the shag tongue!

One April day, in a roadside rain-water pool we saw a merry company of wriggling pollywogs, that were just changing into frogs.   It was laughable to see them, half one, half the other. Soon the pollywog tail and skin will drop off, and, feet coming out, he will graduate from the swimming school and become henceforth a hopper and a croaker.   It is one of the many miracles of nature's mysteries.

In this month, the green of the herbage and the green of the deciduous trees meet and greet each other for one short span.   All the rest of the year they live apart.

Now the large colonies of butterflies leave the coastlands, — I suppose, for the city gardens or the mountain ranges ; they return again to winter.

One of the most interesting sights in our sycamore grove was the annual conclave of hundreds of thousands of large brown butterflies. Within a few days they seem to gather from nowhere, and in countless numbers attach themselves to the hanging boughs and leaves of the sycamore trees. They are so numerous that they will make a tree look dark brown in color, and they are so closely crowded together that they resemble festoons suspended from the trees. During the forenoon hours they will leave the trees for feeding, and the air will be actually alive with butterflies. When spring comes, as if by magic they depart as suddenly as they came, evidently remembering the beautiful trysting-place through instinct, as selected for them perhaps for centuries.

The serene fields of springtime are now receiving their last showers. Late in April falls "the grasshopper rain," as the Mexicans say. It is so called because after its advent the warm spring sun sweats the eggs deposited on the herbage, and thence the grasshoppers soon come forth, a thousand strong in each locality.

These Southern California growing spring days, when the trees are starting in leaf, — can you not remember them ? Not only can you almost see the trees grow, but you can almost feel as if the buds were bursting out on yourself.

Fog effects in May are very beautiful. Sometimes the fog will drift in from the sea over the foot-hills like a gauzy veil, delicately covering the landscape. At times you see its loveliness distinctly, and again, the fog-mist coming between you and the vista of hill-lands, an indistinctness results which seems like that of a dream. Just now the sun bursting through the fog-drift revealed the silvery tops of the olive orchard.

The coming in of the fog from the ocean on a hot August day is as a benediction from Heaven.

Now the golden ears of corn decorate the porch, and bear witness of autumn. The green of the lofty sycamores has turned to russet, and their falling leaves will blanket the tender grasses, against the cold nights ahead. It is pleasant now to lean over the pasture gate, and let the country sun pour its genial warmth on your back.

At this season begin to blow the Santa Annas, the fierce autumn wind storms, — dreaded, to be sure, but zephyrs, compared with cyclones. Three days they blow, and often precede a rain. They are a blessing in disguise, for beside their sanitary, microbe-dispelling effects, they also drive the dormant seeds hither and thither, to distribute them equally on the surface of the land. This task accomplished, down pour the early rains and up come, as by magic, the living green grasses out from the browned hills and fields. With lightened step bring forth the team. Plough and pray. Pray and plough. It is a time of hope. After such a blessing, faith comes easy.

In November fly to our shores the snipe, the ducks and geese from the northlands, furnishing a large food supply, sent yearly by a kind Providence to Southern California. Now fall the quail before the swift-flying shot. The olive tree, a commissariat in itself, gives its bounty. The *citrus* glory begins to appear in the orange groves. An amber comb of sweet cave-honey is on the table. All nature has been teaching the lesson of service. So let each citizen prove some service to God and men, and thus fulfill the mission of life, and make harmony on earth as complete as possible till comes the Christ. "No man liveth to himself alone."

The Chinese say, "Give a man rice, oil, and vinegar, and he has all his system needs for food." Not a farmer of ours but can have the equivalent of these, and how much more! With wheat, corn, or barley he has his cereal, his olive-trees provide his oil, and his vineyard or apple orchard his vinegar. If he lives by the sea, fish may be his; he can have a pig in the pen, and many a thrifty mountaineer makes his poultry produce pay for his groceries. And

it goes without saying, we can all have fruit.
How long before we shall learn to rely upon
a diversity of crops, to raise what we need?
Were men ever so independent as when the
home loom wove the homespun cloth from
home-grown wool from a modest flock?

It is the edge of winter. Can Southern
Californians celebrate Thanksgiving with gratitude, when the barn is full of sweet-smelling
hay, and seed-barley is on hand, with great bat-
tlements of corded stove-wood, sufficient flour,
two noble sacks of beans, a barrel of brined pork
in the storeroom, and plenty of fish in the sea,
while our seine is freshly dipped in tanning?

Now comes winter, the time of short days.
December twenty-first is here, the shortest day.
It has always seemed to me that the New Year
ought to begin with December twenty-second,
when the days commence to grow in length.

When the winter comes, the seals, true to
time, seek our pleasant waters, and you find
them resting on rocks and sleeping with one
eye open, lest both be closed forever by the
cruel bullet. I wonder where the calendar is
printed that tells fish and fowl when to seek
other waters or other climate. Who teaches
them to read it?

It is Christmastide. The bearberry, our
substitute for English holly, has been gathered
out on the hills, and the mantel is prettily
trimmed, while a wreath of it hangs over the

door.   There are hurried footsteps in the morning, each hastening to be first to bid "Merry Christmas" to the others.   There are interchanges of kind words and gifts, if the Christmas Eve tree has not done its duty the night before.   There is the family worship and the singing of old Antioch and Hanover, those two old Christmas hymns so full of glory. Then there is the great Christmas-tide fire, in the broad and deep fireplace ; a real Christmas fire, crackling and roaring in gladness as it offers its tribute of holiday cheer, around which we gather after a happy dinner off a home-fattened turkey, that had unconsciously been preparing himself for us during a fortnight, to keep company with the cranberries from Cape Cod. How proud a man is to dine off what he himself raises !

At the close of day the parents are telling the children that the joy and gifts of Christmas Day would never have been had not God sent Christ from heaven to pilot us there, that we might escape hell.

It has been a great day.   There was the basket to fill and carry on horseback to the neighbor whose stores were scant.   Then there was the dear flag of our beloved country to raise on its staff, and the boys saluted it with cheers and several tigers as it beautified the breeze which unfolded it.   In the afternoon was the stroll, or boat-ride, or mountain climb, or agate search, or the delight of the gun.

Ah, Merry Christmas Day! would that thy joy might be known the world around, — as it will be after Shiloh comes!

THE STORY HOUR

AROUND THE HEARTH

Draw down the shade, shut out the night,
Let in the day of candlelight.
Come round the fire, or take a book;
Be grateful for this ingle nook.

WHAT an advantage it is to have plenty of firewood about; oak-trees growing while you sleep. Look at that oaken back-log, which has been growing fourscore years for you; now on the fire there, it will be consumed in three hours, — just as the three-year-old ox, having developed month by month, is slaughtered and is all gone in a few days. The strength of the oak and of the ox have been converted into human strength. It is a good thing to look ahead to old age, and to see there is plenty of young firewood growing up on the farm against those days.

I like a Southern California ranch that has oaks and olives on it : they express so much.

The oak and the olive
Here grow with great ease;
The one standing for strength,
The other for peace.

But returning to our back-log : what is really

more precious than a fireside ?   Some things
are ; you could count them, however, on your
fingers, and away up high on our list of blessings would be the winter fireplace.   Happy
hours are those passed around the hearth, and
especially delightful are those rare evenings
when the general household seems to be in a
general mood for story-telling.   At such a time
our minds blend in many kindly thoughts and
memories.

THE STORY HOUR

One night the strength of the storm without
seemed to bring us all into close sympathy.
The power of God in the gale bound our hearts
to heaven and harmony.   One of the boys said,
as he put three sticks of buckthorn on the fire : —

"Father, tell us a story, *please*."

"Yes, I will," the latter answered, "on condition that you each tell me one, and that each
shall relate histories instead of stories, — re-
miniscences of the past."

"Agreed, and all right," came the voice
chorus of affirmatives ; "signed, sealed, and
about to be delivered."

"Well," said the father, after he had been
silently collecting all the five-dollar thoughts
which concerned by-gone days, "how would
this arrangement do for the evening's enter-
tainment ?   Suppose I apportion to each of you
and to myself a theme for talk."

All said, "'T is well."

"Therefore, to you, mother, I will assign as a subject some notable remembrances of our humble past. To thee, my son, I give the animal kingdom. For thee, daughter, I choose the birds; tell us of them and their past relations with us. While to thee, namesake, I intrust the ludicrous, and I will help you out in your recollections. It will do us good to laugh to-night.

"Mother, let thy pleasant voice make us forget the storm without. We await thee."

"The most notable remembrances that come to my mind on such short notice are these, — perhaps inspired by the storm, for they chiefly deal with robbers. The fury of the gale sounds as if burglars were seeking entrance through the windows.

"Once upon a time, children, there came to the ranch just at dusk a man, driving an iron-gray horse in a two-wheeled cart. He said he wished to go to Hueneme. Thy father told him there was no wagon road there. He replied he would go as far as he could on wheels, then leave his cart, and proceed on horseback over the mountain trail. He asked to stay the night. Thy father, discerning the man's bad character, gave him sleeping accommodations in Friendship Flat, which was a loft in the calf shed reserved for tramps. The next morning he sought early to leave the ranch without

saying or paying anything.   But a locked gate
intercepted his way, and he had to come back
in front of the house.   He gave us all a sullen
look, and passed on up the grade.   Thy father,
(how, I know not) exclaimed, 'That man, I believe, is the Ontario bank robber who robbed
that bank the other day, and whom the sheriff
wants.'   Well, that man did as he said, reached
Hueneme, and went back to Los Angeles, from
whence he dug up the gold he had cached, and
then abode at a hotel, where, not being able to
restrain his love of finery and jewelry, he was
arrested on suspicion from his abundance of
gold, and was eventually convicted.   When we
saw in 'The Times,' children, the man's por-
trait, and found out *he* was the robber, you can
imagine how strangely we felt over thy father's
exclamation, and over the fact that a bank robber had been our guest in Friendship Flat.

"Perhaps," the mother continued, "I should
narrate how once we were almost swallowed up
in the black bog, when we drove across it to
get a duck that was wounded.   We had not
then known the Octopus-like tendency of that
mire.   We barely lived to tell this tale.   Or,
also, about a grand meteor we once saw in
1894.   This marvelous meteor fell in the early
twilight, when it was still quite light.   After
the red ball fell a large trail was left in the sky
for half an hour.   The color of the trail was
white.   Some said the color was caused by

phosphorus; others said the nickel in the meteoric iron, when in combustion, made fumes of that color. One Alabama observer said he heard the meteor pop, and that he had never seen a trail remain luminous so long. Perhaps in rapid whirl a planet threw off at a tangent a mass of rock.

"But," the same voice said, "I was to talk about robbers. One morning, very early, children, thy father and I had to go to Los Angeles. Three miles from home, down the coast road, we were just driving past a clump of sumacs, when a man sprang out of the brush, and with raised sand-bag, drew himself up to strike us from behind. It so happened, miraculously, that thy father, who had the whip in his hand, whipped up the team at that very moment, and the horses, answering to his bidding, quickly carried us out of danger. We have never since ceased to thank God for our deliverance. Had it not been for that providential fall of the whip, the sand-bagger of our hold-up might have had all our nickels, which were few, and have ended our hopes, which were many."

Thereupon, the children embraced their mother; and soon the father said in judicial tones, "My son, reveal the thoughts of *thy* theme."

"Well," said the son, "since to me it is given to relate memories of the animal kingdom, and since the theme has begun in a domestic way, I may be limited to dogs and cats, chiefly. At all events I will recall to your minds how sad we felt when Republican, our great Saint Bernard, jumped upon our firstborn colt 'First' and bit his leg so severely we feared for his life. How surprised we have been to see him live to draw us after him. And we shall love to remember how Republican's successor, Protector, used to overdo his duties by barking at the scarecrow in our berry-bushes, and by attacking the first bicycle that ever came to the ranch. Of course, he had never seen one before and he concluded it was a dangerous thing to people and property, so he rushed at the bicyclist, nipping at the revolving pedals and boots. It was well for the rider that the great Saint Bernard was soon brought to obey his master's voice. Does any one here know anything more disagreeable than a combination of man, bicycle, and fierce dog all in action?

"Mother, we could never forget dear old Tiger, our house cat! Do you remember how he surreptitiously got into the dining-room at supper-time, and lay down on the electric foot-bell under the table, and how the maid came in to answer the bell? Ah! how sorrowful we were when that very wicked, half-wild black cat would come down from the hill behind the house, and pounce upon poor Tiger, and how we children used to run to his rescue and drive off the marauder. I recollect how Christian, the dairy boy, set the box trap one night to

catch this evil black cat, whom we felt to be
our enemy as well as Tiger's, and how in the
morning we found the trap sprung.   Christian
was almost beside himself over his success as a
trapper, and, leading us to the trap, we all
peered into the box, and from the color and
voice of the wild beast within we, to our sad
surprise and dismay, recognized our fireside
cat, Tiger himself.

"That was too bad when we lost that great
gopher-expert, the cat sent us from The Palms.
Do you remember how in the night I heard its
cries, and how, the next morning, we found it
killed by some wild animal?   How badly we
felt.   And how we did rejoice at the possibility
of the death of its slayer, when our neighbor
the next day rode up the avenue with a large
wild cat or lynx he had shot, and was bringing
as a present to us boys.

"We used to enjoy the little angora kids so
much, father, when you first bought the band
of goats.   That was an amusing sight to see
the little angora who got his head into an old
coffee-pot and ran blindly, hither and thither,
trying to extricate himself.   Do you remember
how brother, by accident, called the herder
Philistine instead of Celestin, his right name?
And how, when one of the silken-haired goats
got lost on the mountain, a man saw it high up
on a pichaco, and sent his trained dog after it?
You know the dog caught the goat, holding it

by the nose till his master came, who honestly brought it to our corral."

"Happy memories of happy days," the mother said; and then the master of ceremonies spoke.

"Daughter, the birds are bidding thee tell something of their past that played a part of our past."

"Then I obey. I will pass by the finding of the poor dead humming-bird in the rose garden, the capture of the wounded eagle, the orioles that built their nest from the ridgepole of our tent, the queer little owl found in the hollow of the oak-tree when it was felled, and how afterward he stared at us out of his screened box. I will merely mention, as analagous to my theme, the discovery in Sweetwater Cañon of an old bird's-nest in a bush, which had been preëmpted by a mouse for his home. Ignorant of its contents we were about to remove it for our nest collection when, presto! out jumped the mouse.

"I remember, father, that day you rescued a poor road-runner from the cruel talons of a hawk; how, though wounded, you brought him home, and we nursed him to life, and let him go because he was a benefactor bird, — an enemy of snakes. We examined his plumage, his long green tail feathers, his purple crest, the red scalp at the back of his head, his long beak, and his wonderfully made feet, the talons of which were in sections and protected with a kind of armor-plate, so that while he wound his claws around a rattlesnake the armor-plate would shield him from the virus. Surely our God wrought a marvel in this bird. Who could doubt the existence of an intelligent, personal God after viewing such an evidence of intelligence in the power that created the bird and so fitted him for his peculiar livelihood? The roadrunner could not have made himself at the beginning of time. No, it was God.

"But you know mother and I have been making a study of hawks. Shall I not tell you somewhat of them? You know how last year our dovecote was besieged by hawks to the death of four pigeons, and how you, brother, took down the 'old reliable' and shot both the cruel hawks. Alas! the slow-flying doves became a ready prey to the wind-swift hawks. Our cote lost many tenants. The dove-colored feathers were sadly numerous here and there.

"We wonder exceedingly at a hovering hawk; as he motionless holds himself high in the air and watches for booty while he scans his surroundings, until, discerning something, with oblique flight he darts downward and strikes with fierce strength the neck of a passing bird, his purpose being to break it, and then devour the bird in a convenient tree. Only yesterday, under the ford oak the fallen feathers strewn upon the ground revealed a recent tragedy.

"And how arrow-like they pierce the air; on pinions swift and strong these prey birds speed along, flying one hundred and fifty miles an hour. The rifleball can easily overtake the hawk, since it goes a thousand miles an hour. But what a slow coach the bullet is when we read that electricity moves 288,000 miles in a small fraction of an hour."

"Why, sister, how much you know," the boys said.

"But what I shall never forget, father," the daughter continued, "was your simile concerning a hawk, one Sabbath afternoon. We were watching some great hawks flying, scooping low along the hillsides after ground squirrels. One way they flew their shadows betrayed them, and revealed their presence to the scattering squirrels, so that the hawks could not make a success of their toil. You know you likened this to anything unkind or wrong that we might do, acting as a shadow on our lives and preventing us from true success. You told us how such a shadow could be obliterated by the power and ability of Christ, but that the only safe way was to always fly in such a righteous direction that no shadow would fall to our injury or defeat."

"What a memory you have, daughter; I shall be very careful what I say hereafter in your hearing. Well, my namesake, there are only two left to end the programme. Wilt thou begin? And I will close with a narrative which I promise you will eclipse your effort to cause laughter."

The son began, saying that, as his subject was given him, he was at the mercy of circumstances, and would have to say that something was ludicrous in Southern California even if it was only to mention the odd little bow of a ground owl, the queerness of a baby horned-toad, or the remarkable assertion of a tenderfoot in the Pullman that Southern California was noted for its real-estate liars and its small stoves.

The lad went on, " You know once, going to San Francisco, a traveling acquaintance told us there was a certain cañon near Mojave called 'Hat Cañon.' It is near the line of the railway. A man dwells there who makes a superior living from the sale of hats. First, be it known, Mojave is the home of the wind. There Boreas was born. The wind blows as nowhere else. Wind-mills there might generate enough electricity to run Niagara Falls. Well, this hat-merchant gathers up all the hats that blow off the heads of the passengers who put their heads out of the car windows, and then sells them to the passengers on the next train, bound the other way, who had lost *their* hats in a similar manner. This the wily dealer repeats *ad infinitum.* He will doubtless soon sell out his interest to an English company, and three per cent bonds will be issued for a vast amount.

"But to come back to our family. Do you remember how we used to give Don Quixote, the donkey, peppermints to eat, to his and our delight, and how he brayed for more? Do you remember, father, how that pet deer, with a red-flannel collar, overtook you on a mountain trail in the north and so surprised you when you turned to see whose footstep it was behind you? And how you were awakened one night by a great buzzing in the room, and thought a bat had flown in through the open window, and how, lighting the candle, you found to your amusement the visitor was only a big, brown butterfly? And how, when you bought the Saint David colt of the Mexican, in reply to your inquiry he said its name was Geronimo? You know you then said, 'Geronimo? Where have I heard that name? I believe it is Spanish for Jerusalem;' and how, afterward, you remembered it was the name of the renegade Apache chief? You said you noticed José hung his head a little when he told you the horse's name.

"It always seems so ludicrous when I recall a certain neighbor's story about a stranger who 'put up' with him over night in his cabin. In the evening the party promised to give his host, for his kindness, an interest in a mine. In the morning our neighbor discovered the stranger

had stolen his revolver. The thief had two
hours' start, but old Nelly was soon loping her
best in pursuit. When at last overtaken, the
stranger refused to give up the weapon, and
even declared he had not taken it. Discretion
was a good part of valor, our neighbor thought,
and he returned to his cañon. Now comes the
amusing part of the story. In relating this
narrative our friend would always end his remarks by earnestly saying, ' Would you believe
it ! to this day that *man* has never given me an
interest in his mine ! '

" You all surely recollect our experience with
those citified staghounds we bought in Los Angeles ; how, when they got homesick, they
ran down to the Southern Pacific train and
jumped into the baggage car ; and how, once
when they pursued some rabbits, they got so
winded we had to bring them home in the
carriage for fear of heart failure. City dogs,
indeed !

" You know that night the deputy-sheriff and
the United States customs officer came to the
ranch, armed to the teeth with magazine shotguns, and went up to the Point to be ready
to seize an expected importation of smuggled
Chinamen ; how their errand was in vain, save
in the discovery of a supposed smugglers' cave
under the cliffs by the sea ; how the cave con-
tained a cooking-outfit, blankets, oil clothing,
and a dark lantern ! Well do I remember the

inscription on a piece of paper, 'Beware! dynamite is hidden here!' Yes, the officers thought, they are smugglers, sure enough; see that dark lantern, — that gives them away! But when they showed me a book of Ballantyne's, 'The Fire Brigade,' and, opening it, I found therein a Christian tract, I said, 'These are no smugglers.' 'Well, what are they then?' replied the officers. It eventually turned out that all of this booty was the result of a wreck on the rocks of a little sloop made and owned by Santa Monica high-school boys, and the dynamite notice was placed there for the purpose of frightening away any gentlemen who might desire to possess themselves of the dark lantern and the frying-pan, before they, the boys, could return to carry home in another boat their cached valuables. You remember, we boys hauled home part of the wreckage of that good ship, the Petrel.

"But, to conclude, I must mention the monkey and the pruning-knife. How, when we lived in Los Angeles, a neighbor's pet monkey came into our carpenter shop, and finding an open pruning-knife, experimented therewith, — to his detriment; inasmuch as he shut down the blade of the said knife upon his fingers so that he himself could not extricate them. His face was a picture of bewilderment and misery. We gave the alarm across the street, and his owner got him out of his trouble.

"Now, father, it is your turn. Can you excel that?"

"Why, certainly, my friends. I am going to tell you a story about a Redondo *mephitis*. You know *mephitis* is the aristocratic name of a pole-cat. Well, once upon a time, when we lived by the side of the fair, pebble-jeweled beach at Redondo we occupied a two-story house on the bluff. We had been annoyed by pole-cats climbing up into the attic. The clothing closets in the rooms upstairs had ventilating apertures in their ceilings, and no screens had been put on them. One fine morning down dropped an inquisitive polecat — no, *mephitis* — into my closet. I heard him fall, and, peek-ing in, shuddered at the thought of my predic-ament. What could I do? Force was out of the question. Diplomacy would be a good thing, but how could I employ it? A butter-fly collector who was visiting us solved the problem. The said collector exclaimed, 'I know how; chloroform him! I have some.' So we tied a string about a vial of chloroform, very, *very*, VERY gently swung it in a crack of the door, which we closed, and awaited the slow passing of fifteen minutes. Then, full of mixed curiosity and alarm, we cautiously opened the door and beheld the polecat insensible! A pair of tongs lifted him up into a five-gallon oil can, and thence he was personally conducted to a barranca near the beach, where I left him.

" Ah me, how can I ever relate the rest ?

" Well, looking out of the window an hour after my return to the house I beheld, to my amazement, the said mephitis walking casually up the slope from the place in which I had put him, and — would you believe it ? — he steered for our front gate, came into the yard, got under the porch, and soon was wending his audible way up to the attic, where he and his friends made themselves obnoxiously at home until we departed to our winter quarters at Los Angeles. They may be there to this day ! "

" Father, the palm is thine," my son shouted. " That story should go to the ' Youth's Companion.' "

And so the evening ended, amid much appreciation of the ludicrous side of life's experiences.

" Good-night, my bairns.   God guard you till the morning."

THE STORM

THE storm was closing in on us. We felt the sullen stillness which oft precedes a gale. Phalanxes of the mighty armed hosts of cloud-land advanced across the skies ; here some awful Krupp thunderhead menaced the position of other clouds ; there some little ones sped like cavalry to the focal point of the battle in high air ; while, yonder, dense ranks of serried clouds covered the heavenly space ; until finally the various forces of the opposing cloud armies were well drawn up, and then came the great attack. The lightning flashed, the thunder-head revealed its power like thundering artillery, while the mass of cloud-troops fired down countless volleys of hailstones. Please accept the preceding photograph of the great storm of January 16, 1895.

Before the storm broke, the scudding clouds fled as if to escape the fury of the approaching gale. A fierce wind foretold the battle ; all nature seemed to cower in fear. The gulls shrieked their alarm. Fright was in the air. The surf beat angrily on the shore and the foam rose high. The trees bent before the blast and the birds lay low. The sharp gusts of wind shook the windows and speckled the panes with raindrops. The farmer gave a final look to the shelter of his stock; his good wife put a stout oak stick on the fire, that a bright warm blaze might cheer her coming husband.

The gale was now in command; we thanked God for a strong house. The storm-king spoke down the chimney. The gutters talked. The house trembled, and an instinctive prayer went upward for ships and men at sea. Ay, 't was a whistling gale, — a pier-breaker!

The terrible velocity and fierceness of that winter wind, accompanied by its shrill shriek, struck terror to the heart, as it beat against the home. The house trembled, but did not collapse, and the fitful gusts, baffled, flew forward to other battles. Ah! it was a good thing to have God that night. The noise was terrific; the blinds blew off. The darkness was illumined by frequent flashes of lightning, and in the midst of the storm's fury, with a hissing sound, a thunderbolt fell near by. It was good to know one's sins forgiven that night. The furious wind seemed to be driving the artillery away, and its rattling reverberations against the mountain walls died off in the distance, when suddenly, as if it had forgotten something, the wind shifted, and again the storm was upon us in increased power, stalking among the high peaks above the foothills. Again fell the hail, and the windows almost yielded to the force. Again and again the lightning gleamed, and the flashes nearly overtook each other in a continuous glare. God seemed to have emptied out the vials of his wrath. The cañon walls echoed back the thunder in defiance of the storm.

When at last the storm abated we went out on the porch. The air was still ploughed by the rapid-falling rain. We heard the sea resounding against the rocks. We left the tempest outside and sought the cheer within. The spirit of the storm seemed to speak, using the chimney as his trumpet, " Cross not the ford to-morrow morn. The river's king am I for five successive days. Cross not, lest horse and man together tangled in the turbid flow shall find their death."

The next morning there came forth the glorious California sunshine, and from the freshly anointed pastures rose the earth vapor. How glad the thirsty ground was to drink in the pelting rains ; one can almost feel as it must have felt. All nature was aglow with gladness.

THE MENTAL CITY

DID you ever, in your mind, build a town, or lay out a city site on land you owned? It is very interesting, — even if it should not come true. About the sitting-room table did your household ever consider that matter, and all agree that John should lead the Christian life of the place, and Douglas should be president of the bank, the best bank of course, and Ruth should teach the school, and every one should have a place? Open sin would be kept out, and happiness would be found in ever so many places beside the dictionary; and lots would be worth so much, and so many at such a price would amount to — dear me, what a prodigious sum! What great good you could do with it!

And then we discussed our city's name. What a task it was, to be sure; what merriment the various propositions caused!

The business member of the group wished our city to be called Port Pasadena, Sunnyside, Summershore, Wonderland, Happyland, Safehaven, Glenhaven, Resthaven, Safeport, Seabright, Stillwater, Bestbay, Billowbay, Bluewavebay, or Stirling. "Take your choice," said he.

The poet wanted the name to be either Foot-hill Park, Mountainside Park or Cañonside Park, Runningbrook, Deerbrook, Seabrae or Braemar, Edgewood, Midocean, Contentment, Peacedale, Waverley, Serenity, Diadem, or Switzerland.   I should have said we had two or three town-sites, in different localities; hence the great variety of descriptive names.   We had not decided which city we would build first, don't you see?

The practical member said, "Oh, let us name it something that means something; let us call it Enterprise or Industry or Recreation."

Hereupon the poet sighed.

And he sighed again when the facetious member remarked, "Why don't you call it Sunshine or Seek-no-further, or best of all, Climate, and then you'll catch the Eastern crowd."

To counteract the uncalled-for levity on the part of this last destroyer of sentiment the classical scholar then said, "Now to give it true dignity its cognomen should be Hygeia Park, Ozone, or Aristos."

Then the member who had been studying Spanish upspoke and said, "It seems to me we should call it Gloriosa or Marina."

The historian slowly said, "Would not history suggest the name Zumaland?"

There was but one more to speak, and he was the student of truth.   Said he, "Among so many it is hard to choose, but there are still

some good ones left.   Permit me to propose
Christland, Palestine, Puritan, Archangel, Evan-
gel, — and Hopehaven for my preference next
to the first ; since there is no hope for man
save in Christ.   Neither is there ultimate haven
for man save in heaven.   Thus the name Hopehaven stands for all that is dearest to mankind."

If you have never laid out a town in your
mind, begin now.   You will never regret it.
Even if the trolley never comes your way, you
will say to yourself, " Well, how I did enjoy my
mental city in anticipation ; the realization could
never have been so joyous, so it is all right that
the plough still turns up my city's streets, and
that those great, tall office buildings are still
only castles in the air."

By all means build a mental city.   That is a
privilege peculiarly Californian.

ON POINT DUMA

The marine freshness of the air at Point Duma is rarely found elsewhere. The atmosphere is so heavily charged with ozone as to make it a valuable tonic and strength-builder. Seen from the high foothills to the north this headland looks like a great sea turtle, its head toward the sea. Its lofty white stratified cliffs, the hard, low-tide sands at its feet, and the quietness of its anchorage make it an attractive locality, while the wooded cañon of Ramirez makes a beautiful park close by, wherein are hidden lovely vistas, most unexpected.

To this anchorage old Captain Phineas Banning used to come to load his vessels with oak wood from the cañon to be taken to San Pedro. The oaks were topped for firewood, and in the interim have regained their growth. This bay is sometimes known as Banning's Harbor. A small breakwater here constructed would make a crowning glory to the other attractions. Deep, unruffled water is near the shore, and no dredging would be needed. Indeed, it is now a safe harbor at all times save when a southeaster blows, which is the rarest of our gales.

Tell me, O Point Duma, of the sights thou

hast seen! Of the first man that ever stood
upon thee; how long did it take thee to get
accustomed to the ways of mankind? Tell me
of the wars of the aborigines or the sea tragedies thou hast witnessed. Tell me of the many
bands of seal of long ago that rested on thy
rocks. Canst thou remember the high-decked
Spanish ship, Cabrillo carrying? And the Boston clippers, hide and tallow traders? Didst
thou see the sail of Sir Francis Drake, while
the canoes, swift paddled, sought the shore in
fright? Thou must have seen the very ship
in which Richard Henry Dana sailed before
the mast. Within thy vision argonauts have
passed, gold seeking. And since then have
moved in review before thee the steam mer-
chantmen and the white navy.

Tell me, Point Duma, hast thou heard the
tales of the silent smugglers? Even now whispers of smuggling debase the air. Yesterday
I saw an ill-looking craft, under the cover of
the drifting fog, crawling up the coast. Her
blackish sails looked piratical. Last night well
armed detectives stayed the night with us, asking for shelter. They were spying out her
landing-place and her movements. The presence of smugglers gives an unpleasant feeling
in the air. Did you see those tracks on the
beach at daybreak? Did you notice where they
led?

Passing vessels used to throw overboard

opium and other articles, and their confeder-
ates would pick them up in small boats. When
the duty on opium was taken off the temptation to make unholy profit was removed. One
man who knew too much of the smugglers'
crimes was found dead ; murdered, the detectives said, to still his voice forever. But God
will avenge.

The Chinese opium-dealers in Los Angeles
were the final recipients of this accursed drug.
To escape detection, opium has been brought
into Los Angeles inside of jew-fish, in trunks
checked as clothing, hidden in planks made hollow to receive it, and in countless ways. It
used to be very difficult to secure the offenders,
owing to alleged connivance in high places.
And, when it is remembered that such cunning was resorted to, that bananas on the
bunches and oranges in the box were found
stuffed with opium, we cannot wonder that the
smuggler has so often escaped. It was esti-
mated that one "ring" in San Francisco had
defrauded the government out of four million
dollars' worth of duties on opium.

Yes, Point Duma, if thou couldst only speak
thou couldst tell us if the claims of the pre-
Scandinavian discovery of our Pacific coast by
the Japanese are true. Long, long before Cabrillo came, it is believed shipwrecked Asiatics
cut inscriptions on the rocks at Sinaloa, on the
west coast of Mexico. The Chinese also claim

historical evidence that their voyagers found our coast centuries before Cabrillo.

But let us leave these echoes of the past, though without the fact the echo could not probably have come; and let us go to that fact which is all written down in good old Anglo-Saxon print, — the fact that Sir Francis Drake of England sailed along the California coast in 1579, and that he landed not far from San Francisco and held Christian services on June 24, 1579, Francis Fletcher being the Church of England priest. To commemorate this first Christian meeting in our beloved California there has recently been erected by the Episcopal diocese of northern California a massive cross, rising fifty-five feet from the ground, the largest in the world. The funds for its construction came chiefly from George W. Childs, the Philadelphia philanthropist.

Sir Francis Drake is believed to have been the first Englishman to stand upon the coast of California. But to Cabrillo, the Portuguese, belongs the honor of having first discovered the coast of California in 1542; he it was who named Cape Mendocino after the Spanish viceroy, de Mendoza, in whose service he was. Although Cabrillo was the first to sail up the coast of California, yet he was not its discoverer; that honor belongs to Hernando de Alarcon, who, in 1540, first came to California by the way of the Colorado River.

It is interesting to know the origin of the word "California." The name was first given, in a Spanish romantic story, to an imaginary island abounding in gold and precious stones. The story was by many people regarded as fact; and, when what is now Lower California was discovered by members of the Cortez expedition, they imagined they were on an island, and as it was apparently very rich, they gave it the name "California."

Ah! Point Duma, thou hast seen history written on the seas, Asiatic, aboriginal, European, American, and only to-day did we together see a fleet of junk-rigged Chinese fishing craft, bound southward; surely a return to first principles and a repetition of history.

What is before thee, Duma? When will the electric lighthouse be built on thy flint foundations, enabling thee to see by night? When will the steam fog-horn disturb thy slumber, and the bell buoys tinkle in the dark? Will not the iron roadway yet compass thy point or pierce thy heart by cruel tunnel? Will the iron horse be contented with steam, or will he feed on electricity, or air compressed? Art thou a prophet?

Whence thy name, Duma?

"My name should be spelled Zuma. It is so called from an Indian tribe whose bodies at my base await the resurrection. Once these seas were not so desolate as when, before the ships of nations came to Port Los Angeles, desolation ruled the deep. Long, long ago canoes well manned by coast-dwellers skimmed the waves with patient paddles, swift, gliding from isle to isle and from settlement to settlement on shore : bent on voyages of trade, of food finding, of ceremony and merciless war, of joyful marriage, and for friendship's sake. But crumbled now are their little ships. Civilization stalks the seas. Nought remains of those days but a shadow of their pristine blood which now flows mingled with the blood of Spain and Mexico."

So "Zuma" is thy name. Methinks in some way it may be allied to Moctezuma the Aztec. He, tradition said, came from the north ; some say the Rio Grande Valley. Thy name is the termination of *his* name. It is a pleasant thought that Moctezuma the great was akin to thy tribe. It may be he had traveled to see the ocean, before he sought the south, to combat Cortes.

What wonder and terror would possess the mind of an aborigine, could he now, like Rip Van Winkle, awake to this marvelous metamorphosis ! What would he think when he saw the mighty steamships blackening the skies with their smoking energy, and landing at the southern piers many a cold-driven seeker of sunshine ! What would he say makes electricity ? It is the transition from drawing fire from rubbing sticks to drawing fire from the skies.

Up the coast, towards Hueneme, there was once a very powerful chief of the Mogu tribe. Other tribes of the Southern California coast paid tribute to him, and at regular intervals a congress of the Southern California coast tribes would be held in his domain, a part of which was what is now the Guadalasca Rancho. He was truly the Grand Mogul of Point Mogu. Tradition says he would furnish supplies to all the delegates of the tribes during the days set apart for the congress, but after that time they had to look after their own commissary department.

THE LAST WORD

I HAVE not mentioned in these chapters things that are generally known; and I have purposely omitted facts commonly stated in books on Southern California, its products, its resorts and comparative climatology. What gain would it be to read what one already knows? Instead I have sought to seek out and to describe matters not so often written about and yet distinctly Californian. It is possible that while reading the previous pages memories of Mount Lowe, of Catalina, and of Coronado have floated across the mind like the mist which floats over the foothills in the spring; if this book has awakened such memories, happy am I.

Kind reader, I hope we may meet again; and, the next time, in a book of *your* writing.

𝕿𝖍𝖊 𝕽𝖎𝖛𝖊𝖗𝖘𝖎𝖉𝖊 𝕻𝖗𝖊𝖘𝖘

CAMBRIDGE, MASSACHUSETTS, U. S. A.

ELECTROTYPED AND PRINTED BY

H. O. HOUGHTON AND CO.

Reprinted by

ANDERSON, RITCHIE AND SIMON

LOS ANGELES, CALIFORNIA, 1972

Reprinted by

KNI, Incorporated

Book Publishers, Anaheim, CA 1984